Vinegar

THE COMPLETE
PRACTICAL HANDBOOK

Publisher's Note:
All possible care has been exercised by the author and publisher to ensure that the tips and remedies included
in this guide are basic, simple and safe. However, it is still important to note that all uses of vinegar should be practised
with caution and a doctor's, or relevant professional's, advice should be sought if in any doubt.

Please note also that the measurements provided in this book are presented as approximate metric/imperial/US-cups equivalents.

This is a **FLAME TREE** book
First published in 2008

Publisher and Creative Director: Nick Wells
Project Editor: Cat Emslie
Photographer: Paul Forrester
Home Economist (and Author): Maria Costantino
Art Director: Mike Spender
Layout Design: Lucy Robins and Mike Spender
Digital Design and Production: Chris Herbert
Picture Research: Helen Snaith

12 11

9 10 8

This edition published 2011 for Index Books Ltd by
FLAME TREE PUBLISHING
Crabtree Hall, Crabtree Lane
Fulham, London SW6 6TY
United Kingdom

www.flametreepublishing.com

Flame Tree is part of The Foundry Creative Media Co. Ltd
© 2008 this edition The Foundry Creative Media Co. Ltd

All pictures are courtesy of Foundry Arts except the following, which are courtesy of Shutterstock: 7 © Igor Smichkov; 10 © Zsolt Nyulaszi;
13 © Natalia Clarke; 14 © Katharina Wittfeld; 18 © Micahel Rubin; 23 © Aleksej Starostin; 29 © Carly Rose Hannigan; 33 © Jennifer Nickert;
39, 109 © Thomas M. Perkins; 49 © DJM-photo; 57 © Jeffrey Van Daele; 60 © C. Docken; 69 © Tischenko Irina; 71 © Sharon Kingston;
72 © Kameel4u; 75 © Jiri; 77 © Patrick McCall; 79 © Gordon Swanson; 82 © Ronald Sumners; 84 © Damian Herde; 87 © Tero Sivula;
93 © Spauln; 95 © Joy Brown; 101 © Scott Bowlin; 104 © Jakub Semeniuk; 107 © Sandra Cunningham; 108 Singh Boparai;
110 © Ximagination; 113 © Khafizov Ivan Harisovich; 115 © Michael Pettigrew; 116 © Gordon Ball LRPS; 117 © Danny Smythe;
120 © MalibuBooks; 121 © Jita; 123, 134 © Liv Friis-Larsen; 133 © Elke Dennis; 141 © Alex Staroseltsev; 183 © Ingrid Balabanova

ISBN 978-1-84786-186-3

A CIP Record for this book is available from the British Library upon request

Printed in China

Vinegar

THE COMPLETE
PRACTICAL HANDBOOK

Maria Costantino & Gina Steer

**FLAME TREE
PUBLISHING**

Contents

Introduction

History

Vinegar has been made and used for thousands of years: in fact, vinegar is the oldest storable food and because it can be stored for an almost unlimited period, it is the only food without an expiry date.

The ancient Babylonians around 5000 BC were among the first to recognize the versatile nature of vinegar and used it as both a preserver and a condiment. They were also the first to flavour vinegar with herbs and spices. The 'Father of Medicine', Hippocrates (460–370 BC) is known to have prescribed vinegar to his patients in order to restore the four humours (blood, black bile, yellow bile and phlegm) to a balanced harmony.

Vinegar is also mentioned in the Bible – in the Book of Ruth and in Proverbs, and it was specified in the Talmud for making *haroseth*, a dried fruit and nut paste eaten at Passover as a reminder of the mortar used in buildings by the Israelites when they were slaves in Egypt.

An Expensive Dish

The Egyptian queen Cleopatra understood vinegar's solvent property: according to Pliny the Elder, Cleopatra bet her lover Mark Antony that she could spend 10 million *sesterces* on a single meal. Antony accepted the bet and the next night was surprised to be served a quite

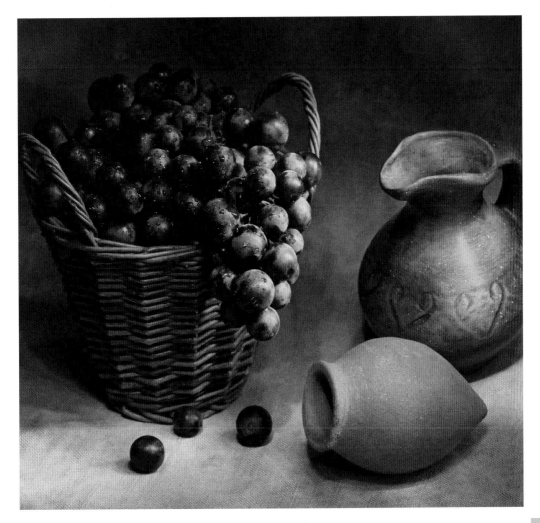

modest meal. He believed he had won the bet when Cleopatra ordered the second course – a cup of vinegar – to be served. The queen, however, removed one of her pearl earrings, dropped it into the vinegar, watched it dissolve and then drank the mix.

A Military Staple

While citizens of Rome enjoyed fine wine, ordinary soldiers had to make do with *posca*, a mix of vinegar and water with a little honey as an optional extra. Vinegar also came in useful *against* the Romans: when the great Carthaginian general Hannibal and his army crossed the Alps on the back of elephants, any boulders that blocked their path were heated and doused with vinegar causing the inconvenient obstacle to be shattered.

Medicinal Use Continues

In the nursery rhyme, when 'Jack fell down and broke his crown' he bound his head with vinegar and brown paper. The therapeutic benefits of vinegar have been known for centuries: in Asia, vinegar is known as the 'friend of Chinese herbs' because it is often used in the preparation of traditional medicines. During the American Civil War, vinegar was used to treat scurvy and as recently as the First World War it was being used in trench hospitals to sterilize wounds.

Whether you call them 'traditional', 'natural' or 'folk' remedies or recipes, today vinegar continues to be one of the most versatile products in the kitchen and medicine cabinet. And, with our growing awareness of the impact of chemicals on our environment, vinegar finds itself once more at the forefront of household cleaning.

Production

Vinegar is nothing more than an alcoholic beverage that has 'gone sour', which explains the French origins of the word *vin aigre*, meaning 'sour wine' – although it was not until 1864 that Louis Pasteur made sense of this natural process of fermentation. When alcoholic beverages sour it is because of the action of certain bacteria, known as *acetobacter*, on the alcohol that turns it to acetic acid and water. Other elements, such as the type of fruit or grain from which the alcohol is originally made, give different vinegars their individual characteristic tastes, bodies and colours.

The Orleans Method

In theory, making vinegar is a very simple process: make some wine (or beer) and expose it to the air for the vinegar bacteria to get to work. The *acetobacter* reaction is an aerobic reaction, and simply requires the presence of oxygen. One of the oldest methods for producing vinegar is called the Orleans process. The 'generator' used is a large wooden barrel that is laid on its side with the bung hole facing towards the top. At each end of the barrel, holes are drilled so that when the beer or dilute wine is put in, the liquid in the barrel is just below the holes. The slow fermentation allows for a non–toxic slime known as the 'vinegar mother' composed of the bacteria and soluble cellulose, to form on top of the liquid.

The barrel holes are covered with fine gauze (to keep out insects) and the 'generator' allowed to sit for several months at around 87°F /29°C. When all the liquid is turned to vinegar, all but 15 per cent is

drawn off through the bottom of the barrel. What is left behind in the barrel is the vinegar mother that becomes the 'starter' for the next batch of vinegar.

The more oxygen available in the process, the faster the vinegar can be made. So, over the centuries vinegar producers came up with a variety of ways of increasing the amount of oxygen in order to shorten the time taken in the vinegar–making process. Today, commercial vinegar is produced using either a fast or slow method: slow methods are used with traditional vinegars and can take several months. A form of nematode, known as a vinegar eel (*Turbatrix aceti*), that feeds on the vinegar mother, can occur in some forms of vinegar – in particular, naturally fermenting vinegar – but most manufacturers filter and pasteurize their vinegar before bottling, thereby avoiding any adulteration.

Speedy Production

The fast methods of vinegar production generally add vinegar mother to the liquid, then introduce air using a turbine or pumping system. Additionally, the generator may be loosely packed with a porous material such as *pommace* (grape pulp after is has been pressed) or beech wood shavings to provide a 'mash' with a greater surface area for the volume of vinegar mother. This method can produce vinegar in 24 to 36 hours.

Activity Levels

The acetic acid concentration of vinegar typically ranges from 4 to 8 per cent by volume for condiment (table) vinegar, though it is usually around the 5 per cent mark. It exists in much higher concentrations for pickling – up to 18 per cent – although in some countries the maximum strength may be less than this as solutions above 10 per cent need careful handling as they are corrosive to the skin.

Types of Vinegar

White Distilled

White distilled vinegar – in fact colourless and transparent in appearance – is also sometimes called spirit vinegar and is made by oxidizing a distilled alcohol made from grain, usually maize. White distilled vinegar is typically stronger and sharper than other vinegars and consequently is most often used in pickling and preserving recipes. Its stronger concentration of acetic acid also makes it a valuable household cleansing agent.

Malt Vinegar

Malt vinegar is made from a grain, typically barley. The barley is first softened by steeping in water and is then allowed it to germinate. This causes the natural enzymes in the grain to become active and start digesting the starch that is converted into maltose, or sugar, before fermentation. The vinegar is then filtered and aged – often for some years – before bottling.

The distinctive flavour of malt vinegar makes it a popular choice for pickling and for sprinkling on fish and chips. A less expensive alternative is 'non-brewed condiment': this is typically a solution of acetic acid and citric acid coloured with caramel. Because it is non-brewed, it is a 'safe' vinegar for those who eschew all alcohol-based products.

Beer Vinegar

Vinegar made from beer, which is technically a malt vinegar, is a speciality of Germany, Austria and the Netherlands and its flavour depends on the type of beer it is made from.

In Bavaria, speciality beer vinegar continues to be made according to the Bavarian Law of Purity of 1516 enacted by Duke Wilhelm IV and which requires all beer and beer products to be made solely of barley, hops and water. Like the beers themselves, continental beer vinegars are lighter in colour than British ales and malt vinegar, although they do all share the distinctive 'malty' taste.

Red & White Wine Vinegar

Wine vinegar is made from either red or white grapes, and like wine itself, it is the variety of grape used that defines the flavour. Also like wine, there are different qualities of wine vinegar available. Generally, the longer wine vinegar is aged, the better the quality – the finest quality often being aged for two years. Because red wine vinegar has a strong, full bodied flavour, it is most commonly used in Mediterranean cookery recipes for marinades and vinaigrettes.

Made from selected blends of white wine, white wine vinegar can vary in colour from 'white' to pale gold. White wine vinegar has an acid content of between 5 and 7 per cent and therefore a sharper flavour than red wine vinegar.

Champagne Vinegar

With a taste similar to champagne, this vinegar is produced using the same grape varieties as the 'king of wines', Chardonnay and Pinot Noir. The same process for making wine vinegar is used, but once the grape hulls are removed and the liquid drained, the end result is a fine vinegar with the rich flavour of champagne along with a hint of vanilla, which comes from the aged oak barrels in which this vinegar is made.

Balsamic Vinegar

True balsamic vinegar comes only from Modena and Reggio in Italy and is made from the juice of Trebbiano and Spergola grapes. The traditional method of production involves an initial fermentation which reduces the volume of the 'juice' by two thirds, and then the thickened 'storm' is placed in the first of a series of five barrels made only of approved woods: oak, chestnut, cherry, ash and juniper. At each barrelling, the volume of liquid has been reduced: from an initial 100 litres (26 gallons), to 70, then 50, to 30 and finally, a mere 10 litre–barrel of dark – almost black – viscous, and sweet–flavoured vinegar.

After five years the first balsamic vinegar is ready, but only balsamic vinegar that has been aged for at least 12 years – and up to 150 years – may be labelled *Aceto Balsamico Tradizionale*. It is this long, slow method of 'hand' production that accounts for the typically high price of traditional balsamic vinegar. Industrialized production using grape concentrate, sugar, caramel (to darken the colour) and wood flavourings make for cheaper, but inferior balsamic–'type' vinegars.

Sherry Vinegar

Like balsamic vinegar, sherry vinegar is a speciality of a distinct geographical region and production method. To be called sherry, the fortified wine may only be made in the Spanish province of Cadiz, and in a defined area between Jerez, Sanlúcar de Barrameda and El Puerto de Santa Maria.

Made in the region since the sixteenth century, the wine must be made by the *solera* system (a fractional blending method) and aged for at least two years. The vinegar itself comes from barrels of sherry that contain too much volatile acidity, so cannot be used for wine. Like balsamic vinegar, the longer sherry vinegar is aged, the finer the quality: 30-, 50- and 75–year-old *reserva* sherry vinegars are highly prized for their rich, mellow flavours.

Apple Cider Vinegar

Made from cider or from an apple must or 'mash', cider vinegar has a strong, acid-sharp flavour at full strength, but when dilute, has a distinctive apple taste. Fast industrial manufacture, which can take as little as 24 hours, often uses concentrated juice from eating or dessert apples with added sugar, rather than traditional Somerset cider apple varieties such as Kingston Black, Morgan Sweet, Sheep's Nose and Yarlington Mill, which are fermented naturally for at least two years. Such cider vinegars are a brownish–yellow colour, and are often sold unfiltered and so contain vinegar mother.

Rice Vinegar

Rice vinegar is a speciality of China, Japan and Southeast Asia and comes in white (actually a pale yellow), black and red varieties. White rice vinegar is made from fermented rice, although a variant with a stronger taste and often called seasoned rice vinegar, is made from Japanese rice wine or *sake*.

Black rice vinegar, usually made from sweet black rice but which can also use millet and sorghum, is a dark brown colour and has a distinctive smoky taste, while red rice vinegar is made from fermented red yeast rice and has a sweet but salty flavour which makes it ideal for use in sweet–and–sour dishes and dipping sauces.

Fruit Vinegar

Fruit vinegars are made from fruit wines with no other flavours added – not to be confused with non–fruit vinegars infused with fruit or with added fruit flavours. The most common fruit vinegars are those made with raspberries, blueberries or blackberries, which are consequently sweet and delicately flavoured. Many fruit vinegars are specialities of Europe, although fruits such as persimmon and apple–flavoured *jujube* (Chinese date) are used in Korea and China.

Raisin Vinegar

This cloudy brown, mildly flavoured vinegar is sometimes also called grape vinegar – raisins are after all, dried grapes. Raisin vinegar is produced widely in Greece and Turkey.

Date Vinegar

We know the Babylonians in around 5000 BC were making vinegar and it was most likely made from dates, the only available staple foodstuff for the inhabitants of desert and arid regions. Both these vinegars are popular in Middle Eastern cuisine.

Umezu

The famous Japanese 'pickled plums' (actually apricots!) called *umeboshi* are the source of *ume* vinegar or *umezu*: the fruits are picked when ripe, packed in barrels with salt and a weighted lid placed on top. Gradually, the *ume* plums give up their juice and the salty liquid is drawn off and marketed as *umezu* or vinegar.

Coconut Vinegar

Used extensively in Southeast Asian cooking, especially in Thai cuisine, and made from the 'tuba' or 'toddy' – the sap of the coconut palm – coconut vinegar has a low acidity, a slightly musty flavour and a unique aftertaste. The sap is naturally fermented into vinegar over 45 to 60 days, then bottled. Unfiltered and unpasteurized coconut vinegar contains vinegar mother, and as it ages in the bottle the colour changes from cloudy white, to light yellow, to clear light brown, although filtered and pasteurized versions are available.

Cane Vinegar

In the Ilocos region of the northern Philippines where this vinegar is traditionally made, it is known as *sukang iloko*. Outside of the Philippines, it is often labelled as *sukang massim* which simply translates as 'sour vinegar'. Although it is made from sugarcane juice, it is no sweeter than other vinegars and has a rich, sharp flavour that makes it ideal for pickles and sauces.

Corn Sugar Vinegar

Corn sugar vinegar is the result of alcoholic and then subsequent acetous fermentation of corn sugar. It has a smooth, mild flavour and distinctive amber colour.

Honey Vinegar

Honey is often added to vinegar – especially cider vinegar – to enhance the flavour, but vinegars made from honey are also produced, particularly in France and Italy.

Fermented honey, water and yeast was used for thousands of years to make a traditional wine called mead and the resulting honey vinegar is gold coloured, lightly flavoured but highly aromatic.

Kombucha Vinegar

Sometimes called 'pro-biotic vinegar', kombucha vinegar is made from a colony of yeast and acetic acid bacteria which forms into a 'mat'. This culture also goes by the acronym SCOBY (Symbiotic Colony of Bacteria and Yeast) and was originally made into fermented 'tea' during the Qin Dynasty in China around 250 BC and used extensively in traditional Chinese medicine.

Each time the kombucha colony is fermented, a new colony is produced and forms a new layer on top of the mat. After three or four layers have built up, the 'tea' becomes sour and tastes like vinegar. Both the kombucha tea and the vinegar have recently become very popular on account of their alleged therapeutic properties.

Flavoured Vinegars

Flavoured vinegars are, as their name implies, vinegars that have had flavours added to them rather than made from them. Generally the 'base vinegar' is a red or white wine vinegar in which fruits such as raspberries, lemons, oranges (especially the deep red blood orange) and even figs, have been infused. Herbs and spices are also popular flavourings: thyme, oregano, rosemary, tarragon, basil, mustard, chilli and garlic can all be used. (*See* pages 132–35.)

Laundry

Stain & Odour Removal

The level of acetic acid in white or distilled vinegar is strong enough to dissolve the alkalis in soaps and detergents, but not strong enough to harm fabrics. It also has bactericidal properties. Consequently, white vinegar is a valuable 'green' alternative to synthetic chemical cleaners and when it is diluted with water, which further reduces the risk of damaging delicate fabrics, it is also a very economical one.

Cleaning Clothes

Pre-Wash Stain Removal

White vinegar is such a useful pre-wash stain remover it is worthwhile keeping a spray bottle with a half-and-half solution of white vinegar and water close to hand. As you check over garments before putting them in the washer, treat any heavy grime or underarm perspiration stains with a quick spray of vinegar.

Wine Stains

Wine stains can be removed from cotton and cotton polyester fabrics – but only if you get to the stain within 24 hours! Here you do need to use undiluted white vinegar: sponge it gently on to the stained area and blot with a clean cloth. Repeat until as much of the wine stain as possible has been removed and then wash according to the care label instructions for the garment.

Deodorant Stains

Antiperspirants and deodorants can leave horrible white marks on clothes. These can be removed by lightly rubbing white vinegar on them and then laundering as usual.

Soak Away Bloodstains

Bloodstains are quite easy to remove before they have dried and set into fabric but are nearly impossible to shift after 24 hours. If you can get to the bloodstain quickly, pour undiluted white vinegar directly onto the spot and let it soak in for 5–10 minutes before blotting with a clean cloth. Repeat if necessary and then launder as usual.

Unset Old Stains

Older, set-in stains can be successfully removed by treating the affected area with a solution of 3 tablespoons white vinegar, 2 tablespoons liquid detergent and 1 litre/2 pints/4$\frac{1}{2}$ cups warm water. Repeatedly sponge and blot the stained area and then launder.

Collars and Cuffs

Collars and cuffs are particularly vulnerable to stains, especially greasy ones from perfumes (sprayed on the pulse points of the neck and wrists) and from make-up.

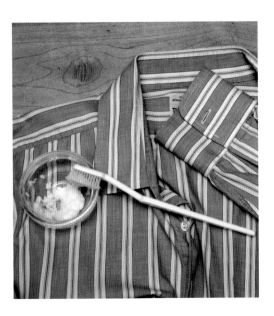

Make a paste of 2 parts white vinegar and 3 parts bicarbonate of soda and use a soft nail brush – or a discarded and recycled toothbrush – to gently brush the paste into the soiled cuffs and collars. Let the paste set on the fabric for half an hour and then launder as usual. This technique is also good for removing mildew spots from vintage fabrics.

Ink Spots

The primary carrier for the colour in ball-point and roller-ball pen inks is a very fine oil – often castor oil – so ink marks can be treated with white vinegar, which cuts through the grease and lets the colour flow off the affected fabric.

Treat the ink stain first by blotting with undiluted white vinegar, and then gently rub in a paste of 2 parts white vinegar and 3 parts corn flour. Let the paste dry completely on the ink stain and then launder as usual.

Better than Bleach

Greying white socks, and even dingy face flannels can be made brighter and given an antibacterial treatment: place about 1.7 litres/3 pints/7¼ cups cold water and about 145 ml/5 fl oz/²⁄₃ cup white vinegar into a large saucepan and bring it to the boil. Put the dingy socks – or face flannels – into a bucket and pour the boiling vinegar solution over them. Let them soak overnight and the next day, launder them as usual.

Restore Whites

White garments or fabrics that have yellowed can be returned to their former glory by soaking them overnight in a solution of 12 parts warm water and 1 part white vinegar and then laundered the following day as usual.

Vintage Lace Restored

Old and antique lace is often very delicate so start any cleaning process by soaking it first in cold water and letting it dry naturally.

If it is still on the yellow side when dry, use a very mild solution of white vinegar and water: 24 parts water and 1 part white vinegar for an overnight soak. Rinse well and allow the lace to dry naturally – in the sun if possible, as this will also help in the 'bleaching' process.

Odour Removal

Banish Smells From Suits

A night out can leave your clothes smelling of stale cigarette smoke or even the smell of the food you ate in the restaurant. You can, however, often remove the odour from clothes without resorting to dry cleaning. Put 145 ml/5 fl oz/²/₃ cup white vinegar in the bathtub and fill the tub with hot water. Hang the offending garments in your bathroom and close the door and let the 'vinegar steam' impregnate and deodorize the garments for a couple of hours. Afterwards, hang the garments in an open space – not the wardrobe – to let them 'dry out'.

Second-hand Smells

Scouring vintage and second–hand clothing stores can yield fashionable finds, but even though the garments may have been cleaned, they can often have lingering odours. Add 120 ml/4 fl oz/¹/₂ cup white vinegar to the wash cycle – or to a bathtub of water if the garment is vintage and needs delicate hand washing. This will deodorize the garment, and kill off any bacteria that may be present.

Clean Machine

You will not get clean clothes from a dirty washing machine, so once in a while, pour in about 230 ml/

8 fl oz/1 cup white vinegar and run the washer on a full cycle but without clothes or detergents. This will clean out residual soap scum, remove mineral deposits and deodorize your washing machine.

Kill Bacteria

Because of the acetic acid content, white vinegar has bactericidal properties and so about 120 ml/4 fl oz/½ cup white vinegar added to your washer's rinse cycle will kill off any bacteria present in the wash load, especially if it contains terry diapers (or sweaty sports socks). White vinegar will naturally break down uric acid from baby and children's clothes.

Colour
& Condition

White vinegar is not just a 'greener cleaner' but

is useful for keeping the colour fast in garments

and linens. It is also a great way to put the 'bounce'

back into fibres as it acts like a fabric conditioner.

The acidic nature of the vinegar cuts through

grease and the alkalis that form the base

of many soaps and detergents.

Improving Condition

Blanket Reviver

Cotton and wool blankets and bedding can be revived and made soft and fluffy – and free of soap residues and odours – by adding about 230 ml/8 fl oz/1 cup white vinegar to the final rinse cycle.

No More Fabric Softeners

Unless you happen to like your laundry smelling of synthetic perfumes, there is no need for expensive fabric softening liquids or sheets (the latter are also partly responsible for 'furring up' the heating elements of washing machines causing them to overheat and break down!). Instead, try adding 120 ml/4 fl oz/$^1/_2$ cup white vinegar to the final rinse for soft and fresh-smelling clothes.

Lint-free Laundry

If your clothes are emerging from the wash covered in lint do not despair. Next time, add some white vinegar to the final rinse and you will find them lint free – and static free too.

Banish wrinkles

Sometimes clothes have wrinkles and creases that have dried in: this can happen even when they are brand new from the store. Rather than iron them out, de-wrinkle them by hanging the garment on a clothes hanger and lightly spraying a mist of a solution of 1 part white vinegar and 3 parts water. Let the garment air dry.

Keep Woollens in Shape

If a sweater has emerged from the wash and appears to have grown by yards, do not despair. Make a solution of 1 part white vinegar to 2 parts warm – not hot – water and soak for 20–25 minutes. Gently squeeze out the excess, but do not wring the garment as you will only twist the yarn and stretch it further. When you have squeezed as much water out as you can, lay out the sweater flat on a large folded-up towel and gently arrange the sweater back into shape. Put another towel on top and gently blot the sweater, letting the towels absorb more moisture. Put the sweater flat on a new, dry towel and let it dry naturally.

Shiny Seats

The seats of skirts and trousers can become shiny, even after a single wear. Dip an old, but clean, toothbrush into a solution of equal parts white vinegar and water and gently brush the shiny area. Blot the moisture with a clean towel and let the garment air dry.

Suede Stains

Grease spots on suede garments, shoes and handbags can be removed if you dip a clean toothbrush into neat white vinegar and very gently brush the spot. Do not scrub or you will damage the nap. Let the spot air dry then brush with a suede brush and repeat if required. Suede items can be revived generally by a gentle wipe over with a sponge dipped in white vinegar.

Salt Marks

Shoes and boots are so easily spoiled in winter when the roads have been gritted with rock salt. Not only does this leave an ugly tide-mark on footwear, but the salt can cause leather, suede and fabric to crack if it is left on. As soon as you can, wipe off fresh salt stains on shoes and boots with a sponge dipped in undiluted white vinegar and let the shoes dry naturally.

Colour Maintenance

Keep Colours Fast

New and old coloured garments can loose much of their colour in the wash and you can end up with faded or streaky patches. To fix the colour, soak coloured fabrics and garments for a few minutes in a bowl of diluted white vinegar before you wash them.

Stop Red Running

Red is a notorious colour for running in the wash and turning everything washed with it pink: but pre-soaking a new red item in undiluted vinegar before the first wash can limit the amount of red dye that is shed. It is still a good idea to wash dark and coloured items separately from white items, but you will find the red items do not loose as much of their colour in the long run.

Bright White, Sparkling Colours

Whiter whites can be had without the use of chlorine beach or the expensive 'bleaches' designed for coloured garments – use white vinegar in the rinse cycle instead. The effect is the same: it fixes the dye, cleans, deodorizes and softens all in one treatment.

Ironing

As the final stage in the laundry process, ironing gives garments the finishing touch. Remember though that there are two ironing techniques: the first is truly ironing, where the sole of the iron is passed gently across the top of the garment to remove creases, and the second is pressing, where the sole of the iron is pressed onto the garment to bring it back into shape and 'iron in' creases. In either case, white vinegar can have a part to play.

Flush Out Your Iron

Clean out your steam iron by filling the reservoir with undiluted white vinegar. Place the iron in an upright position, switch it on to the steam setting and let the vinegar steam clean the interior for 10–15 minutes. This will get rid of any mineral deposits and help prevent the insides corroding. Next, repeat with clean water to flush out any leftover vinegar.

Spotless Sole

Take a look at the soleplate of your iron: are there black scorch marks? If there are, you can guarantee that the next time you iron your favourite garment, these will get deposited onto the fabric! When the iron is cold, scrub the soleplate with a paste made of equal parts of warmed white vinegar and salt and then clean off with a cloth dampened in clean water.

Remove Scorch Marks

Small slight scorch marks on clothing will often come out if you rub the spot with a clean cloth dampened in white vinegar and then blot with a clean cloth, repeating if necessary. This technique can also work on rust spots too!

Stay Sharp

Some garments demand razor sharp creases so use a spray diffuser with a solution of equal parts white vinegar and water and lightly spray the garment before ironing. For some reason, the creases are even sharper if you place a piece of brown paper on the garment and iron onto this rather than directly onto the fabric. Try it for yourself!

Cleaning

All-Purpose Solutions

As a cleaning substance white vinegar makes an excellent, economical and eco-friendly alternative to many chemical cleansers. The acetic acid content is enough to cut through grease and grime, but it also bactericidal, making it effective against most moulds, bacteria and germs. Here you will see a varied selection of basic all-purpose solutions and tips.

All-Purpose Metal Cleaner

Go to the household store and you will find an expensive array of different scourers, polishes and cleaners labelled for chrome, steel or copper. There is no need to spend money on different products when you can make an effective all-round metal cleaner yourself for a few pennies – and be safe in the knowledge that you are not harming the environment.

Mix a tablespoon of ordinary cooking salt and flour (self raising or plain!) with a little white vinegar to make a paste. Work the paste around the surface to be cleaned then rinse with warm water.

Brass, Pewter and Copper Polish

Make metal ornaments and door furniture shine by polishing with a mixture of 2 tablespoons tomato ketchup and 1 tablespoon white vinegar. Rub on with a cloth until bright and shiny.

Cleaner for Gold Jewellery

There is no need for expensive cleaners, just submerge gold jewellery in apple cider vinegar for 10 minutes, then rinse off and dry. *Note: this is only suitable for plain gold items, not jewellery set with gemstones!*

Remove Candle Wax

Candles give a gorgeous light and scented candles are a wonderful way to perfume a room. Apart from the fire risk, the only other problem with candles is that they can splutter molten wax onto walls and furniture.

Rather than scrape off the wax with a knife or blade, which may damage the surface underneath, heat it gently first with a hair dryer and blot up as much molten wax as you can with paper towels. Next, tackle the greasy marks by mopping them with a clean rag soaked in a solution of equal parts white vinegar and water and then blot with a clean, dry cloth.

Un-stick Stickers

Trying to remove the stuck-on price tags from new china and glassware – or from any other object – is probably one of the most frustrating and time consuming activities on the planet. You can peel, poke, and rub away and still there are bits that will not shift.

Thankfully there is a straightforward method: saturate the sticker with undiluted white vinegar and scrape it off. Do not use your fingernail: it will only break! Try using a plastic knife for small, delicate objects so that you do not scratch the surface, or an expired credit or phone card for larger surfaces.

If there are any sticky leftovers, saturate again with vinegar and wipe clean with a cloth. This method works equally well for those sticky decals that are popular with young children and notices on car windows left by traffic wardens.

Greasy Door Handles

Wipe over door handles and knobs using a spray of equal parts of water and white vinegar. It cuts through grease and kills germs too.

Kitchen

Cooking is a messy business but kitchens need to be clean and hygienic in order that food prepared in them tastes delicious and is safe to eat. The anti-bacterial properties of vinegar make it an ideal surface cleanser for food preparation surfaces: undiluted white vinegar at 5 per cent acidity is effective against *E. Coli*, *Salmonella* and *Staphylococcus*, so make vinegar part of your cleaning routine.

Kitchen Items & Surfaces

Clean China and Glass

Make your dinner service sparkle by adding a splash of white vinegar to your rinse water or dishwasher.

Cloudy glasses can be made clear again if you soak them for 10–15 minutes in a solution of equal parts hot water and white vinegar and scrub with a soft bottle brush.

Tea- and coffee-stained cups and mugs can be restored by scrubbing with equal parts vinegar and salt followed by a rinse in warm water.

Grease Stains

The reason we sprinkle vinegar on our fish and chips is not just because it tastes good, but because it cuts through the grease making the food easier to digest.

Tackle grease marks and splatters on surfaces around the home with a cloth dampened in a solution of equal parts of white wine vinegar and water. Not only will it get rid of the grease, the vinegar will also remove any lingering 'fatty smells' – once its own scent has evaporated.

Cutting Boards

Vinegar is effective against harmful bugs such as E. Coli, Salmonella and Staphylococcus, so clean down wooden and plastic cutting boards, butcher blocks and non-marble counter tops where food preparation takes place with undiluted white vinegar before and after use.

If wooden surfaces need deodorizing after, sprinkle them with bicarbonate of soda and spray on some vinegar. Let it foam for a couple of minutes, then rinse with clean water.

Grill Pans

It is the grease that has dripped from food into the grill pan that smells when you next heat the grill up. Too much accumulated grease in a grill pan can also catch fire! Lining the pan with cooking foil is one way of keeping an eye on things, but even then you still need to clean out the pan to get rid of spill, splatters, odours and bacteria.

A solution of equal parts of white vinegar and warm water should do the job, but for really greasy pans, use neat vinegar or make a paste of vinegar and salt or bicarbonate of soda and get scrubbing.

Can Openers

Ever looked really close at the sharp point of the opener or at the cogged wheel? Be horrified at the amount of gunk that is lurking there! Every time you open a can some of that gunk will end up deposited on the surface of the food inside the can! Clean and disinfect your can opener by immersing it in undiluted white vinegar and scrubbing the mechanism with a re-cycled toothbrush.

Clean and Deodorize Food Containers

Plastic food containers, lunch boxes, bento boxes and vacuum flasks can be stained and scented by strong foods and liquids. Wash food containers in a solution of equal parts white vinegar and water, and then rinse clean. Store with the lids off. If odours persist, place a slice of bread soaked in white vinegar in the food container (lid on) overnight: the smell should have gone by the next day.

Fresher Flasks

Vacuum flasks can get stained and smelly so clean them out regularly by filling with warm water and 120 ml/4 fl oz/½ cup white vinegar and letting them sit for a couple of hours. Any residue can be 'scoured' away by adding a small handful of uncooked rice. Put the lid on the flask and shake well, then rinse and let it air dry.

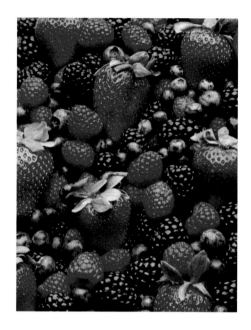

Berry Stains

Preparing soft fruits can leave your hands – and food preparation surfaces – stained. Washing surfaces, bowls and hands with white vinegar and rinsing well with water afterwards will remove the stains.

Disinfect Dishcloths

Cleaning a surface is useless if the dishcloth, sponge or brush is itself dirty. Soak them after each use in neat white vinegar and hot water for a few minutes, then rinse and let dry.

You can also soak loofahs and natural bath sponges in vinegar to clean them of soap residue. Rinse them off with clean water then revive them with a soak in a salt–water solution (which removes any 'slime') before giving them a final rinse in cold water.

Appliances

Fresh Fridge

Equal parts of white vinegar and water make an effective and safe cleaner for both the inside and outside of fridges. If you have got mould or mildew lurking in shelves and fridge drawers, zap them with undiluted white vinegar. An egg-cup-full of bicarbonate of soda placed in the fridge will help absorb odours too!

Kettle De-scaler

Lime and mineral deposits that have built up in kettles – and in coffee makers – can be shifted by boiling up – or brewing up – enough white vinegar to fill the pot to 3/4 full for five minutes. Leave the vinegar in the kettle or coffee maker overnight then rinse out with cold water.

Clean Dishwashers and Microwaves

Once a month, remove soap build-up from dishwashers by pouring 120 ml/4 fl oz/$^1/_2$ cup white vinegar into the bottom of the unit – or placed in a bowl on the top rack. Run the machine on full cycle without dishes or detergent.

Steam clean and deodorize your microwave with a shallow bowl of equal parts vinegar and water and set on high for 5 minutes. When cool, use the solution to wipe away splatters from the inside surfaces.

Bathroom

Relaxing in a tub of bubbles at the end of a
hard day or waking up with an invigorating shower
should be a pleasurable experience in pleasant
surroundings. No matter how old your bathroom
and its fittings, keeping it clean, bacteria and odour
free will add to your sense of wellbeing.

Shower Curtains

After a shower, spread the shower curtain open across the rail to let it dry off. If mildew has stained the curtain, wash it in warm water with equal parts laundry detergent and bicarbonate of soda, then rinse with 120 ml/4 fl oz/$^1/_2$ cup of white vinegar added to the rinse water.

If you use a washing machine, take the curtain out before the spin cycle so it does not crease. Hang the curtain back up and let it air dry.

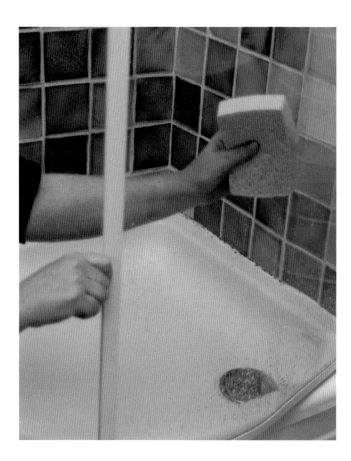

Shiny Showers

Soapy watermarks are unsightly on shower cubicles and screens, and if you live in a hard water area, they can be permanently etched into the 'glass' and ruin its clean looks. At the end of your shower, wipe them down with a solution of equal parts water and white vinegar. Finally, remove all traces of water and vinegar with a squeegee, and leave the shower door open to air dry.

Tackle sliding shower door tracks by pouring in neat white vinegar to clean and disinfect. Leave it to sit overnight then mop out with a dry sponge. For really gruesome tracks, get scrubbing with a re-cycled toothbrush.

Tiles

Soap, shampoo, shower gel and bath foam inevitably get splashed on tiles. Bring dull tiles back to brightness by washing them with a solution of 120 ml/4 fl oz/$^1/_2$ cup white vinegar in 1 litre/2 pints/4 cups warm water.

Grout

Tile grout loses its whiteness and turns grey with age and dirt over time, but its rough surface and porous nature also makes it an ideal home for bacteria to thrive. A re-cycled toothbrush or nailbrush dipped in neat white vinegar will kill germs, and whiten the grout.

Sinks and Tubs

To remove tide marks in your basin or bathtub, try filling with hot water to a level just above the mark and adding a generous amount of white vinegar. Leave it to soak for a couple of hours. Drain away the water and the marks should be much easier to scrub away.

Unclog Plugholes

If not flushed through, soap, shower gel and bath oil residues can build up in the plug hole – more so if there are hairs in there too! Use a funnel and pour 4–5 tablespoons bicarbonate of soda into the plughole. Next, pour in 120 ml/4 fl oz/$^1/_2$ cup white vinegar and watch it foam and fizz.

When the fizzing stops, flush through with very hot water. Wait five minutes then flush through with cold water. As well as clearing the blockage, you have also killed and flushed away any odour-creating bacteria that were hiding there.

Shift Minerals from Shower Heads and Taps

Lime scale deposits can quickly clog up the holes in shower heads: this means that water can back up in your pipes and it puts pressure on your hot water system. Hand-held shower heads can be immersed easily in a deep bowl of white vinegar and very hot water and left to

sit there. The vinegar will dissolve and shift the mineral deposits.

Fixed shower heads – as well as bath and basin taps – are a bit more tricky: fill a plastic bag with neat white vinegar and fasten it with tape, string and rubber bands over the shower head. This works for taps too, but you can also try fixing a plastic cup over the end! Let the tap sit in the vinegar for an hour or so, then rinse off with cold water.

Toilet Bowls

An effective and economical way to keep your toilet bowl disinfected without using dangerous chemicals is to pour about 600 ml/1 pint/2½ cups white vinegar slowly over the sides of the bowl last thing at night. A once-a-week treatment should also help keep away those marks that appear just above the water line in the bowl.

Furnishings & Surfaces

Before mass-produced, industrial chemicals were made available to the domestic market, home-owners made use of natural, organic products that cleaned, protected and polished their furnishings without spending a fortune or harming the environment. Antique furniture and furnishings have lasted for so long looking beautiful because they were cared for very simply, using the most basic products.

Note: Vinegar – and other acidic products – are NOT recommended for marble. This natural stone is made of calcium carbonate deposits and is 'soft', so its polished surface can be damaged even with the most 'mild' acid. Even wine glasses placed on a marble surface can etch rings, so use coasters!

Furniture

Scratches in Wood

Unsightly scratches on wooden surfaces can be disguised using a little white or apple cider vinegar mixed in a jar with some iodine. Adjust the colour to match the wood – more vinegar for light woods, more iodine for dark woods – and paint the scratch mark carefully with an artists' paint brush.

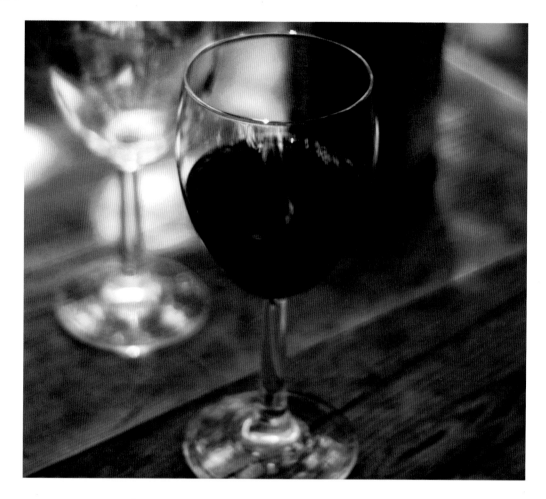

Water Rings

A wet glass on a wooden table inevitably leaves a white ring mark. These can be removed by a mixture of equal parts vinegar and olive oil and applying it with a soft cloth. Do not rub in circles, but move the cloth along the grain of the wood. Use a second clean cloth to polish up to a shine.

Wax and Polish Build-up

When furniture polish or wax builds up on surfaces you can remove it easily and without damaging the underlying wood with a mixture of equal proportions of white vinegar and water. Dip a cloth into the mix and wring it out well, then, moving in the direction of the grain of the wood clean off the polish. Wipe dry with a soft clean cloth.

Leather Furniture

Unsightly white water marks on leather furniture can also be removed by dabbing them with a sponge dipped in undiluted white vinegar.

Leather that has lost its shine can be revitalized with a mixture of equal parts of white vinegar and boiled linseed oil (available form art shops and hardware stores). Put the solution into a spray bottle and spray onto the leather. Spread it over the surface gently with a soft cloth and give it a minute or so to nourish the leather, then buff with a clean cloth.

Leather-topped tables are best cleaned by wiping with a soft cloth dipped in a solution of 2 parts water and 1 part white vinegar and dried off with a soft, clean cloth.

Windows

Let There Be Light

This is the tried and trusted method for getting windows (and mirrors) squeaky clean – it is also cheap and it keeps flies away too! Mix up equal parts of water and white vinegar in a spray bottle. Spray onto the glass and clean off the dirt with scrunched up newspaper. Finish off with a light polish with some brown paper.

Paint Splashes on Windows

Dribbles of dried–on paint on windows look unsightly but can be hard to remove without scratching the glass. The easy solution is to 'paint' on undiluted hot white vinegar onto the mark and give it time to soften up before scraping off with a razor edged tool.

Venetian Blinds

The horizontal slats of plastic or wooden Venetian blinds are notorious for collecting dirt, dust and grime. Wearing a cotton glove – or even an old sports sock placed over your hand – moistened at the end with a solution of equal parts white vinegar and warm water, run your hand across both sides of the blind slats to clean. You will be amazed at how much dirt is removed, so periodically you will have to rinse out the glove.

Floors

Carpet Stains

Some carpet stains can be removed with a paste made from 2 tablespoons white vinegar and 4 tablespoons bicarbonate of soda or ordinary cooking salt. Test on an inconspicuous part of the carpet first for colour fastness, and if it is safe, gently work the paste into the stained area: do not rub outwards as this will spread the stain, instead work from the edge of the stain towards the middle. Let the paste dry and the next day vacuum or brush up the powder residue.

Vinyl and Lino Floors

Bring the shine back to a vinyl floor without making it slippery by washing it with a solution of 120 ml/4 fl oz/$^1/_2$ cup of white vinegar to each 4-litre/gallon bucket of water. Many stains can be safely removed from linoleum floor covering by applying a splash of white vinegar, sprinkling bicarbonate of soda on top and rubbing gently. Rinse clean with water afterwards.

Odours & Pest Control

An often difficult task is trying to 'clean the air' of stale smoke and food odours; conventional chemical room fresheners simply mask the smell and are often overwhelming in themselves. Worse still, they simply shout out loud that your home smells and you have tried to hide the fact! Sniff out smells and deal with them using some simple solutions.

Smoke and Cooking Smells

Burned your dinner? Fried some fish? Had a great party? Banish lingering smells by placing bowls of neat white vinegar around the house. Smells will disappear in a day.

Clear cigarette smoke from the air by flapping a tea towel moistened in white vinegar around the room!

Preparing fish and strong smelling produce like garlic and onions can leave your hands – and food preparation surfaces – smelly. White vinegar will remove the odours from surfaces, but before you handle fish or cut vegetables, try wiping your hands with vinegar first, it will make it easier to remove the odour afterwards.

Freshen Closets

A musty smelling closet needs cleaning and airing out – otherwise your clothes will smell the same! Take out all the contents of your closet, and then, wearing rubber gloves to protect your skin, wash down the walls, ceiling and floor with a cloth dampened in a solution of 120 ml/4 fl oz/¹/₂ cup white vinegar, 120 ml/4 fl oz/¹/₂ cup ammonia and 4 tablespoons bicarbonate of soda mixed in a bucket with 4 litres/1 gallon of water. Let the closet dry out completely before returning the contents.

If a smell persists, try placing a tray of clean cat litter on the floor to absorb the scent – and any residual moisture – and replenish every couple of days until the odour has disappeared.

Deodorize Footwear

Training shoes can be particularly smelly, so try this tip. Most sports shoes are machine washable, so before you put them in the machine, soak them for a few minutes in a bucket with a solution of equal parts white vinegar and water. This will deodorize them and kill any bacteria that have taken up residence. Do the same for sports socks too, and check out the Health & Personal Care section for advice on 'fungal feet' to break the vicious cycle of foot odour.

Missing the Point

Vinegar breaks down uric acid so is a great way to deal with little accidents. Clean, disinfect and deodorize urine–splashed surfaces with a solution of equal parts white vinegar and water. Then sprinkle the area with bicarbonate of soda and let it dry. Brush or vacuum the powder residue after it is dry to the touch.

Fruit Flies

Eating five portions of fruit and vegetables a day is highly recommended, but that can mean a lot of fresh produce ripening in your kitchen, and a welcome sign for fruit flies to come in and dine. Forget chemical fly–sprays; make a simple, eco–friendly fruit–fly trap: half fill a conserve jar with apple cider vinegar, punch a couple of holes in the lid, screw it on and leave it for the flies to end their days in. Every so often, empty the vinegar away and give the flies a 'decent burial'.

Look What the Cat Dragged In

If Kitty has been hunting and brought home a mouse, clean the area thoroughly with neat white vinegar after you have retrieved the mouse remains. If it smells a little 'mousey' still, a neat trick is to lay a paper towel on the spot and put a dollop of washing–up liquid, shower gel or even shampoo on it.

Home Improvement

Plaster, Wallpaper & Paint

We now know that many of the chemical compounds found in many commonly used paints, adhesives and solvents are harmful to our environment, especially if they are disposed of into water courses or buried in landfill. However, we often forget that their use in our homes means that we are in constant touch with them and that some continue to leach noxious fumes into our immediate living environment. So before you reach for the synthetic chemicals, try the natural vinegar solution.

Pliable Plaster

To keep plaster 'wet' for a little longer while you work it smooth on walls, add
2 tablespoons white vinegar to the plaster mix. This will slow down the hardening
process and give you a little more time to achieve the perfect, smooth finish.

Strip-ease

Stripping off old wallpaper is a messy job and can be expensive if you have to hire or buy a
steam stripper. Before you spend your money, try spraying the wallpaper until it is well saturated
with a solution of equal parts water and white vinegar, then scrape away.

If there are tough areas, try scoring the wallpaper with a sharp blade before soaking.
Shifting as much wallpaper as possible this way means you are less likely to fill up your
home with condensation.

Sticky Fingerprints

The acid in vinegar cuts through grease so it is a good cleaner for surfaces (like staircase walls where sticky hands have made a trail) prior to painting, especially if you are using a water–based emulsion: paint over oily or greasy marks and they will 'float' to the surface of your new paint, just like an oil and vinegar salad dressing that has 'separated'.

Restore Paintbrushes

Do not discard synthetic bristle brushes that have dried–on paint. Instead, soak them in undiluted white vinegar until the paint dissolves. Brush handles usually have a hole in them:

thread a skewer or long nail though the hole and balance the brush on the edge of jar, so the bristles are suspended in the vinegar and that way you will not get bent bristles.

Bring Brushes Back from the Dead!

If the above vinegar remedy still leaves your paintbrushes looking beyond all hope, before you consign them to the DIY graveyard try this: bring 115–230 ml/4–8 fl oz/¹/₂–1 cup white vinegar to the boil in an old saucepan and immerse the bristles in the boiling solution for 10 minutes. Then wash with warm soapy water and rinse clean.

Remove Paint Fumes

Even today's water–based and 'green' paints still have a paint odour: always make sure that when you decorate, the room is well ventilated. At the end of the job you can get rid of lingering paint smells by placing a couple of shallow bowls of neat white vinegar in the newly decorated room.

Squeaky Clean

Mildew and dust can be a problem in older properties and during renovation. Wiping the walls with undiluted white vinegar will 'kill' mildew and dampen down the dust making removal easier. For hard to reach ceilings, try using a sponge mop on a pole!

Woodwork, Brickwork & Cement

Vinegar solutions for preparing wood, stone, metal and brick surfaces are cheaper, safer and more ecologically sound than many chemical preparations. Safe as it is, do be sensible especially during prolonged use and rinse your hands to remove any residual acid. Note that even dilute vinegar solutions are NOT recommended for use on marble surfaces as it is easily etched by even very weak acids and can be ruined!

Cutting Edge

Rusted saws and the blades of cutting tools can be 'sharpened' by immersing the metal in undiluted white vinegar for a couple of days. Loosen up corroded nuts and bolts in the same way, and paint vinegar onto rusted screws and hinges before you try to undo them.

Wonderful Wood

Stripped wood in all its natural beauty looks wonderful but can become dull with dirt. Taking off the dirt does not mean you have to take off a layer of wood as well – as you would with an electric sander or stripper.

Before you go down the electric route, try a simpler (and less noisy) solution: mix 600 ml/1 pint/2$\frac{1}{2}$ cups of warm water with 4 tablespoons white vinegar – or even cider vinegar – and 2 tablespoons olive oil in a sealable bottle or jar. Give it a shake and then apply to the wood with a clean cloth. Let the 'dressing' soak into the wood for a few minutes and then buff to a shine with a dry cloth.

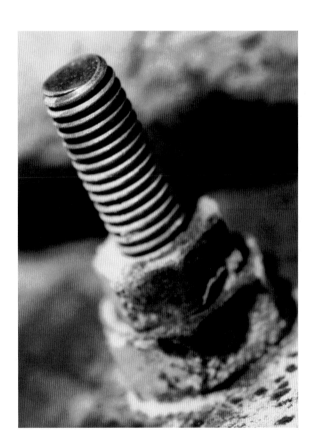

Bright Bricks

Attractive brickwork, whether on floors, walls or fireplaces can often be marred by white or green salt 'tide marks' called efflorescence. This occurs when the mortar or masonry units dry out and the soluble alkaline salts migrate to the surface. Washing away with water can work for a while, but more often than not it brings more salt to the surface.

To stop the problem recurring try washing brickwork with an acid solution to neutralize the alkaline salts: 230 ml/8 fl oz/1 cup white vinegar in a bucket of warm water may just do the trick.

Painting Cement

Light grey cement may not be your favourite finish, so enliven it with colour. Painted cement, however, does have a tendency to peel after a while, but by painting the cement first with an initial coat of white vinegar and letting it dry, you will find that the paint adheres for much longer. You can also use this technique for painting galvanized metal.

Avoid Concrete and Cement Burns

We often think that only heat and acid cause burns, but strong alkalis can also cause skin blistering. It is the lime in concrete and cement mix that is highly alkaline and contact with the skin should be avoided as it can cause skin cracking and even eczema. Wash dried concrete and cement off your skin with undiluted white vinegar to neutralize the lime, then wash in warm soapy water.

The Outdoors

Gardening

Vinegar has a number of herbicidal and insecticidal uses in the garden and because it is made from natural organic products you will not be harming the environment with chemicals. The vinegar that is available for household use does not normally exceed 5 per cent acetic acid, but stronger vinegars for use specifically as herbicides can be purchased. Solutions of over 10 per cent acidity can be 'corrosive' to skin, so make sure you handle them with care.

Improving Soil & Plant Growth

Acid or Alkaline?

Some plants like an acid soil, some like it alkaline and some – like weeds – just do not seem to care either way. Find out if your garden soil is alkaline by placing a handful of soil in to a container, and then pour on 120 ml/4 fl oz/¹/₂ cup white vinegar.
If the soil fizzes or bubbles, your soil is alkaline. If you have a large garden, try the test using soil from different spots to see if it is alkaline throughout.

To test for an acid soil, mix a handful of soil with 120 ml/4 fl oz/ ¹/₂ cup water and 2 heaped tablespoons bicarbonate of soda. Any fizzing and bubbling this time tells you that your soil is acid.

While you now know what kind of soil you have, to find out the exact pH levels, you will need a simple testing kit from a garden centre.

Increase Soil Acidity

Some plants, such as azaleas, gardenias, hydrangeas and rhododendrons, thrive in acid soils. Keep an eye out for yellowing leaves on these plants as this could be signalling a lack of iron or a shift in the soil's pH level above 5.0. If you live in a hard water area, the acidity levels in your soil might be low.

To bring the acidity to a comfortable level for these plants, add 230 ml/8 fl oz/1 cup white vinegar to a each large bucket of tap water, and water once a week for three weeks. The acetic acid in the vinegar will release the iron in the soil for the plants' use.

Blooming Marvellous

With shop–bought bouquets you get a little sachet of plant food, but flowers cut from the garden are effectively put on a starvation diet! They will keep for longer if you place into your vase 2 tablespoons sugar and 2 tablespoons white vinegar for each litre/2 pints/4$\frac{1}{2}$ cups water. Trim the flower stems and change the 'feed' every four to five days.

Speed Up Sprouting

Some seeds, especially the woody seeds of plants such as gourds, passionflowers and morning glory can be given a helping hand to germinate if you rub them gently between two sheets of fine sandpaper and then soak them overnight in a solution of 600 ml/1 pint/2$\frac{1}{2}$ cups warm water and 120 ml/4 fl oz/$\frac{1}{2}$ cup apple cider vinegar.

The next morning, take the seeds out of the solution, rinse them off, and plant them. Herb seeds can also be difficult to get started, and the same technique – but without the sandpaper massage – will help.

Disease, Weeds & Pests

Rust, Black Spot and Powdery Mildew

Before you buy chemicals from the garden centre, reach for the cider vinegar. Mix 1 tablespoon apple cider vinegar with 1 litre/2 pints/4½ cups water and decant into a spray bottle. Spray the vinegar solution onto the affected plants in the early morning or early evening when the temperature is relatively cool and there is no direct sunlight on the plants. Repeat until the condition is cured.

Banish Weeds

Dandelions spoiling your lawn? Banish them by spraying with undiluted white vinegar. Break off the flower head and spray the stalk and around the base of the plant in order to soak the roots. If it rains in the night, go out and spray again! The same treatment also works well for getting rid of grass on driveways and paths.

Keep Off the Grass!

There are many visitors to our gardens who are more than welcome, but there are some whom we wish would stay away. Many animals, including cats, rabbits and deer, cannot stand the smell of vinegar even when it is dry. So to stop neighbours' cats using your borders as a lavatory, and rabbits and deer dining on your vegetable patch, soak some rags in neat white vinegar, and tie them to some sticks or staves. Once a week, soak the rags in vinegar again to keep up the scent.

A 'Friendly' Fly Trap

Gnats, midges, flies and mosquitoes can all be shown the door using a simple organic trap. Take an empty plastic water or pop bottle and pour in around 120 ml/4 fl oz/½ cup apple cider vinegar, about 4 tablespoons sugar, and 120 ml/4 fl oz/½ cup water. Next, cut up a banana skin into small pieces and put them in the solution and shake well.

You can either tie a piece of string around the neck of the bottle and hang it from a tree branch, or place it on the ground: either way hungry flies will make a beeline for the free lunch inside, but have great trouble exiting the neck of the bottle once there.

Give Ants their Marching Orders

An army of ants marching across your picnic table – or a child's play blanket spread on the grass – are a nuisance. Ants, however, hate the scent of vinegar, so pour or spray white vinegar around an 'exclusion zone' and they'll stay clear.

Get Rid of Mealy bugs

Mealy bugs are one of the most common pests to be found on houseplants and in the greenhouse, where they feast on plant juices and can cause leaf drop and subsequent plant death. Look under the leaves and at the junctions with the stem: if you see these small scaly insects, then dab them with a cotton wool ball soaked in white vinegar. The vinegar will kill them – and any eggs they may have laid.

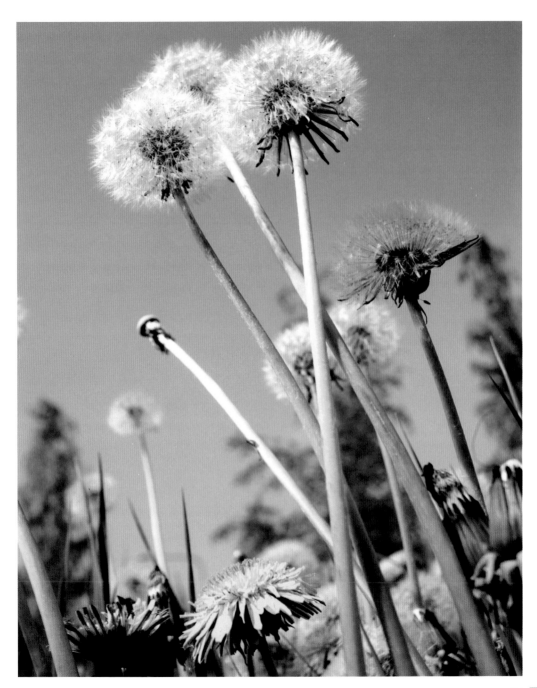

Home Exteriors

When the sun comes out there is no better place to be than outdoors, especially if it is as comfortable and clean as indoors. Check out the home improvement section for useful tips for renovations, repair and decoration and make sure you have your vinegar handy for the following uses.

Garden Furniture

Furniture and Decks

Wooden garden furniture and decking are
very attractive additions in any outside space,
but they do need regular maintenance.
In warm, damp conditions mildew can be
a problem so have a handy spray bottle of
full strength white vinegar to hand. The
mildew will wipe off quite easily and the
vinegar will keep it from coming back for
a while. For large areas such as decking,
use a brush and a bucket.

Shining Shades

Fabric patio umbrellas and awnings are
also prone to mildew, especially if they
have been stored closed through the winter.
These can be cleaned and deodorized using
a mix of 230 ml/8 fl oz/1 cup white vinegar,
2 tablespoons washing-up liquid and a
bucket of hot water. Put your gloves
on and scrub. Rinse off with clean water
and open the umbrella or awning to let it
air dry – preferably in the sunshine!

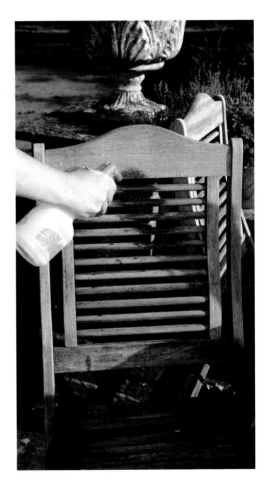

Around the House

Drains

Nothing spoils a sunny day in the garden more than the smell of drains wafting in the breeze. A simple combination of vinegar and bicarbonate of soda is not only the most effective way to clean drains, gullies and waste water pipes, it is also gentler on the pipes and your purse! Use a funnel and pour 2–3 tablespoons bicarbonate of soda down your sink plug hole followed by 120 ml/4 fl oz/½ cup white vinegar. When the fizzing stops, flush through with hot water. Wait five minutes then flush through with cold water.

Fresher Bins

Outdoor rubbish and wheelie bins should be given the same care as the one in your kitchen. When the bin has been emptied, give it a wash with a solution of 230 ml/8 fl oz/1 cup white vinegar, 2 tablespoons washing-up liquid and a bucket of hot water. Pour the solution into the bin and using a long-handled brush or stiff broom, give it a scrub – inside and out. Rinse out with clean water to leave it clean and odour free.

Watch the Birdie!

Messy wet droppings will disappear if you spray them with full strength white vinegar and wipe them off with a rag or paper towel that can be disposed of afterwards. When dried guano is scraped off surfaces it turns into a fine powder that can be breathed into the lungs, so if you are cleaning up dried on droppings, spray them well first with vinegar to damp them down, and do wear a protective mask.

Automotive Care

On the Road

If your windscreen gets more blurred when it rains and you have turned the wipers on, then your wiper blades are dirty. Clean them off by running a cloth soaked in white vinegar along the entire length of each blade.

Organic De-Icer

Most drivers keep a noxious can of aerosol, chemical de-icer in the car in winter and probably throw it away come spring. Save your money, and a space in the landfill site, by spraying your car windows with a solution of 3 parts white vinegar and 1 part water. You will find that it can keep frost from forming on your windows for up to two weeks.

Clean Machine

Shaking out and vacuuming car mats will remove loose dirt, but will not remove stains or smells. Deodorize car mats and remove salt deposits with a solution of equal parts white vinegar and water and sponge it on. Leave it to sink in for a few minutes then blot up with sheets of newspaper or paper towels and let them air dry. You can also spruce up the seat upholstery in the same way, but you will need to do this on a warm day, and leave the windows wide open so it can dry out completely.

Animal Care

Cleaning & Odour Control

Vinegar has a vital role to play in pet care, from keeping their living, sleeping and nesting areas clean and odour free, to keeping out unwanted pests such as fleas and ticks which can affect the health and wellbeing of our animals. Here we see how to minimize smells and keep our animals clean.

Sweet Dreams

You would not be comfortable in a dirty bed and neither will your pet. Wash their blankets as normal but add 230 ml/8 fl oz/1 cup white vinegar to the cycle to deodorize and kill bacteria. Dogs and cats can, like their owners, suffer from sensitive skin: the vinegar will remove any remains of soap from their bedding to which they may be sensitive.

Accidents Happen

House training a kitten or a puppy needs patience – and vinegar – as they will wet any previously spoiled spots because it is marked with their scent. As well as cleaning up, it is vital to remove the scent from the floor, carpet or upholstery.

For carpets, rugs and upholstery, blot up as much of the stain as possible with paper towels, then pour undiluted white vinegar over the spot and blot again. Reapply the vinegar, blot and let it air dry.

For wood and vinyl floors, test an inconspicuous area with a solution of equal parts white vinegar and water to make sure it does not damage the floor's finish. If satisfactory, mop the floor and dry with a cloth or paper towel. In both instances the vinegar will remove the scent so the place will not be 'marked' again.

Feathered Friends

No animal enjoys eating or drinking from a dirty table, so before you fill up the bird feeder with seeds or the bird fountain with water, give them a clean. Empty out any leftovers from seed holders and immerse them in a bucket of hot water and 230 ml/8 fl oz/1 cup white vinegar. Let them sit in the bucket until the water is cold, then rinse really well with cold water.

For bird fountains, pour in a solution of 2 parts white vinegar and 1 part hot water and if possible, give the inside a good scrub. Empty out the solution and rinse really well with clean water.

Dinner is Served

While dogs tend to eat their food in one sitting, cats like to graze. In either case, their dinner bowls can often hold the scent of their food, so after every feed, wash their bowls, then deodorize them with a solution of equal parts white vinegar and water and rinse well in clean water. Remember that cats loathe the smell of vinegar, so make sure Kitty's bowl is well rinsed.

Health & Behaviour

Just as we humans have our 'ups and downs' so too, do our pets. But while we can articulate our woes in words, our pets rely on us their owners to make sure they are feeling good. Like us, pets should have regular health checks. Vinegar can be a handy tool in the first line of defence for your pet's health.

An Apple a Day...

Vinegar is acid until it enters the body, where it becomes alkaline and lines the intestines where bacteria such as *E. Coli* can no longer attach themselves. A teaspoon of apple cider vinegar added to your dogs' drinking water will keep their insides in top condition.

Tick Tactics

Fill a spray-bottle with equal parts of water and white vinegar and apply directly to your pet's coat, rubbing it in well. This may take some doing with a cat because they absolutely hate the smell of vinegar, but then it seems, so do the ticks and fleas!

Bites and Stings

Dab a dilute solution of apple cider vinegar and water onto bee stings and mosquito bites to relieve itching.

Hear Kitty Kitty!

If your cat – or dog – has been scratching at their ears more than usual, a clean-out with a ball of cotton wool or a soft cloth dabbed in a dilute solution of 2 parts apple cider vinegar and 1 part water will clean them and deter ear mites. *Warning: do make a visual inspection of your pet's ear first; do not apply the vinegar even in dilute form to open scratches or sores.*

This is NOT a scratching post!

Cats absolutely hate the smell of vinegar, even after it has dried, so a little neat, white vinegar dabbed onto the proposed scratching post will thwart them!

Health & Personal Care

Apple Cider Vinegar

'An apple a day keeps the doctor away.'

This old rhyme does contain a great deal of truth: like many fruits, apples contain vitamins, minerals and other antioxidant properties which may help to reduce the risk of cancer by preventing DNA damage. Boron, the mineral that is found in apples, may retard bone loss in women after menopause and possibly help women on oestrogen replacement therapy keep the oestrogen in their blood stream for longer.

A Multipurpose Natural Remedy

In recent years apple cider vinegar has become one of the most popular 'natural remedies' for a whole range of ailments. There have been scientific studies and medical trials supporting some of this vinegar's benefits in our diet: it can reduce cholesterol and 2 tablespoons (30 ml/$\frac{1}{8}$ cup) added to our diet has been shown to reduce the GI (glycaemic index) of carbohydrate food. Potassium, which is found in apple cider vinegar, is vital to good health: a potassium deficiency can cause a variety of conditions including hair loss, brittle nails and sinusitis.

Vinegar also contains malic acid, which has been found to destroy micro-organisms including fungi and bacteria – which is why it has for thousands of years been used for pickling and preserving foods. Scientists now know that vinegar also inhibits the growth of gram-negative bacilli (the most well known of which are the bacteria *E. Coli* and *Salmonella*) and because it balances the acid levels in the body, vinegar can help keep the levels of gut flora such as *Candida albicans* in the digestive tract at healthy levels: low acid levels can encourage the growth of fungal infections such as *candidiasis* (also known as 'thrush').

A Reliable Remedy?

Many of the claims for vinegar's curative properties, including 'miraculous weight-loss vinegar diets' and 'cures' for arthritis (involving drinking a mix of honey, apple cider vinegar, water and kelp three times a day) remain untested and unproven, but incredibly popular nonetheless and with a great deal of anecdotal support. Many advocates of apple–cider–vinegar 'cures' claim the acidic content of apple cider vinegar 'breaks down fat', supposedly leading to weight loss, and that the malic acid dissolves uric acid deposits that can form around joints and cause swelling and pain.

Most champions of 'vinegar treatments' recommend apple cider vinegar, but to be truly effective this must be made from fresh, organic, crushed apples that are allowed to mature naturally in wooden barrels. Such 'raw' or 'natural' apple cider vinegar can be found in most good health food shops and should have the vinegar mother clearly present as sediment in the bottom of the bottle. Distilling or pasteurizing apple cider vinegar will have removed not only the vinegar mother, but destroyed many minerals and trace elements including potassium, phosphorus, sulphur, magnesium, iron and copper. Also destroyed in pasteurization are malic and tartaric acids that may be beneficial in fighting toxins and inhibiting bacterial, yeast and fungal growth in the intestinal tract.

Some Drawbacks

While there are no long-term side effects to ingesting apple cider vinegar in moderation, the big drawbacks to drinking substantially larger quantities of vinegar than what you would eat in the form of salad dressing are the strong taste and the potential deterioration of dental enamel. This can give your teeth a yellowish appearance and make them much more sensitive to heat and cold. Some suggest apple cider vinegar is made more palatable by mixing it with apple juice, or with bicarbonate of soda which neutralizes the acid to between 6.0 and 7.0 pH.

Be Prepared

If you are going to try apple cider vinegar for remedial purposes, it is also recommended that you carry out an investigation of your own by buying a pH-testing kit (you can purchase these at a local pharmacies). You can test your urine to see if you are more alkaline or acid so that you can adjust the amount of apple cider vinegar doses. You should also start with a thorough, in-depth investigation of the literature available in books and online, in tandem with a consultation with your medical practitioner. *Do not attempt self-diagnosis or self-treatment: always seek qualified advice for any medical condition.*

The majority of the remedies suggested in the following section use apple cider vinegar (or in some instances white vinegar) as external applications: the nearest any vinegar will get to your mouth is in the form of a mouth wash, and like any other mouthwash, you spit it out after gargling! If you are going to 'eat' vinegar, then it should be a pleasure – as part of a delicious and nutritious meal – so check out the Cookery & Recipes section.

Ailments & Problem Conditions

Before we had medicine cabinets stuffed full of cough, cold and flu remedies, pills, powders and capsules, we would have looked to nature for remedies for our ailments. It is now acknowledged that many 'folk remedies' can be effective to varying degrees. Apple cider vinegar is one such natural product that has recently been 'rediscovered' and found to be effective in offering relief from a range of symptoms of common illnesses and infections.

Flu & Cold Symptoms

Sinus and Chest Congestion

Congestion caused by a cold or sinus infection can be eased by a 'steam treatment'. Put 120 ml/4 fl oz/¹/₂ cup white vinegar into a heatproof bowl and pour on some boiling water. Breath in the steam–vapour. A towel over your head to keep the steam 'focused' will help.

Tight Chests

An old folk remedy for chest pains and 'aching ribs' caused by a cold, flu or by coughing is to soak a piece of brown paper in apple cider vinegar, then sprinkle one side of the wet paper liberally with pepper. Place the paper pepper side down against your chest and leave it there for 20–25 minutes.

Asthma

There is no medical proof that this vinegar remedy works, but many asthmatics swear that pressing cotton pads soaked in vinegar to the inside of their wrists gives them relief!

Sore Throats

A 'raw throat' from singing, talking or after a cough, can be soothed by gargling with a mix of 1 tablespoon apple cider vinegar and 1 teaspoon salt dissolved in a glass of warm water. Use several times a day if needed.

For sore throats associated with colds and the flu, mix equal amounts of cider vinegar and honey, stir or shake until dissolved, and take a tablespoon every four hours, letting it 'dribble' down the back of your throat.

Skin Conditions

Varicose Veins

Again this is not a cure, but is better described as 'relief': soak some 'bandages' made from clean cotton fabric in vinegar and wrap them around your legs – not too tightly – and lie down for 30 minutes with your legs comfortably supported so your feet are above the level of your head.

Corns and Calluses

Corns are hard little 'mountains' formed by increased growth of the skin on toes and are often caused by wearing shoes that are too tight. Calluses are areas of skin that have become toughened through repeated contact or pressure and are most common on the hands.

A traditional remedy for both these problems is to saturate a slice of stale white bread in white vinegar and let it soak for 30 minutes. Then break off a piece of bread large enough to cover the corn or callused area. Keep the poultice in place with a gauze bandage and leave it on overnight.

The next morning the callused skin should have 'dissolved' and a corn should be easier to remove. Older, harder corns and calluses may need a few treatments.

Wart Remover

Warts are caused by a viral infection, specifically by the *human papillomavirus*. One folk remedy is to soak the wart for 20 minutes each day in white vinegar, followed by a gentle rub with an emery board, until it disappears. You could also apply a vinegar–soaked cotton pad and bandage this to the wart.

Cold Sores

Cold sores are caused by a viral infection (known as *herpes simplex* type 1) and are small, painful fluid–filled blisters on the mouth or round the nostrils. Once you have had a cold sore, the virus lies dormant in the nerves or skin around the original site until something – a cold, the flu, stress or generally being 'run down' – causes another outbreak.

You can sooth the pain and swelling, and perhaps 'disinfect' the sore by dabbing with a cotton wool ball soaked in apple cider vinegar three times a day.

Pimples and Spots

Spots and pimples are caused by excess sebum (the natural oil excreted by the skin's sebaceous glands) that blocks up the pores and hair follicles, leading to blackheads and whiteheads.

Apple cider vinegar can help clear the complexion by balancing the skin's pH level and absorbing excess oil from the skin. A dilute solution of 1 part apple cider vinegar and 3 to 4 parts water applied three times a day to the skin and left there for 10 minutes or so before rinsing off will help clear the complexion.

Athlete's Foot

Medically known as *Tinea Pedis*, you do not have to be an athlete to suffer from this fungal infection. It commonly affects the feet but it can be spread – on bath towels – to other parts of the body (especially the crotch) because the fungus needs a nice warm, moist and dark place to thrive!

Keeping feet (and other 'bits') dry, and going barefoot whenever possible, are recommended, but to get rid of the fungus itself (and ease the itching) rinse your feet three or four times a day with undiluted apple cider vinegar.

To guard against re-infection, soak your socks (and jocks!) in a solution of 1 part white vinegar and 4 parts warm water for 30 minutes before laundering them.

Sunburn

Cool sunburn by gently dabbing the affected area with a cotton ball or a soft cloth saturated with white or cider vinegar. This treatment is most effective if you can treat the burn before it starts to sting.

Diaper Rash

You do not actually need to be a baby to get diaper (nappy) rash, although it is babies who are usually associated with this redness and scaling. It is caused by cloth that has been rubbing against the skin for too long, fitting too tightly or been left on for too long. Irritation is also very often caused by the soap residues in cloth nappies and underwear: rinse these in a mild solution of water and white vinegar – about 120 ml/4 fl oz/^{1}/$_{2}$ cup to 2.3 litres/4 pints/9^{2}/$_{3}$ cups of water to neutralize the alkaline of the soap and balance the pH level.

Itchy Skin

The temptation when you get an itch is to scratch, and so break the skin. Insect bites are a common cause of itchiness but a paste made from vinegar and cornstarch will help reduce the urge to scratch.

For overall dry and itchy skin, 2 tablespoons vinegar added to your bath water will help soothe the itch and, being more relaxed, it should also make you less 'antsy'.

Vaginitis

Normally, bacteria belonging mostly to the *Lactobacillus* family live harmlessly in the vagina and produce chemicals that keep the vagina mildly acidic. Vaginitis is the inflammation of the mucosal lining in the vagina commonly caused by a yeast infection.

Add 700 ml/1^{1}/$_{4}$ pints/3 cups cider vinegar to a hot bath and soak for 20 minutes, spreading your legs to let the water flow into the vagina. A return to normal acidity helps banish *candida*, *gardnerella* and *trichomonas* (single–cell anaerobic parasites that infect over 180 million women worldwide each year).

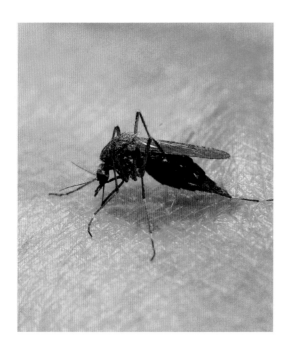

Mosquito Bites

The whining buzz of a mosquito in your ear is in fact the love song of the male mosquito and while the noise may drive you mad, you can take heart in knowing that he will not bite. It is the female mosquito who is the silent blood–sucker and leaves behind her calling card of a nasty, incessant itch, which if scratched too hard can break the skin and lead to an open wound and infection.

Alleviate the itch with vinegar. Not only will it calm the itch, but many claim that the scent of vinegar keeps the mosquitoes from coming back for a second helping.

'Vinegar for Vasp' Stings

Use this simple mnemonic to remind you how to treat a wasp sting: their sting is alkaline so is neutralized by the acetic acid in vinegar. Remove the stinger by scraping the blunt edge of a butter knife in the opposite direction to the point of entry into the skin. A ball of cotton wool soaked in vinegar and applied to the stung area should reduce the pain and inflammation.

If you have any redness and/or swelling 24 hours after being stung you may have an infection, so consult a doctor. If you have had a severe reaction to a sting or bite in the past, you should consult your doctor about the need for an emergency syringe of epinephrine to be carried at all times outdoors.

Aches & Discomfort

Sore Muscles

After a workout in the gym, a day in the garden or a long day's work, treat your aching muscles to a soak in a pleasantly hot tub with 120 ml/4 fl oz/¹/₂ cup of cider vinegar added to the bath water.

Better Digestion

The acetic acid in vinegar is said to help prevent the naturally important hydrochloric acid, which is vital in the process of food digestion, from leaving the stomach too quickly. Food is digested more completely with less 'reflux', belching, 'wind' or indigestion pains.

Instead of a chemical indigestion remedy, 1 teaspoon apple cider vinegar mixed with 1–2 teaspoons honey in a glass of water may do the job just as well.

Hiccups

Medically known as *singultis*, hiccups are caused by a sudden spasm of the diaphragm which causes air to be rushed into the lungs, leading the epiglottis to close – which is the 'hic' sound in the hiccups.

A bout of hiccups normally resolves itself, but an old remedy that claims to 'cure' hiccups is a teaspoon of apple cider vinegar. Rather than any medicinal properties in the vinegar effecting a 'cure', it is more likely to be the sour taste – making your screw your face up and hold your breath – that does the trick!

Improving Appearance

The astringent and toning qualities of vinegar – particularly apple cider vinegar – have for centuries been used as part of women's – and men's – beauty regimes. Vinegar is much more astringent than ice and will reduce inflammation, redness, bruising and swelling in about half the time.

Note: do not apply vinegar – even in dilute solutions – to broken skin (grazes, scratches and cuts) and if you have sensitive skin, rinse off immediately. The acidic nature of vinegar means that you should not apply it to your eyes.

Skin

Age Spots

Age spots, caused by hormonal changes, and sun spots due to over-exposure to the sun, can often be successfully remedied by dabbing with full-strength apple cider vinegar applied with a cotton wool ball for about ten minutes twice a day.

Often the spots will fade in a few weeks, but if they worry you or you notice any significant increase in size or darkness, consult your medical practitioner.

Broken Veins and Bruises

As a gentle astringent, apple cider vinegar is a useful treatment for those tiny, but unsightly broken veins that can often appear on the surface of skin. Dab on undiluted apple cider vinegar to speed the repair and reduce redness. Bruises can also be treated in the same way.

Skin Toner

The use of vinegar as a skin toner dates back to the ancient Egyptians. After cleaning your face, rinse with a basin of cool water with 1 tablespoon apple cider vinegar. You will notice any residual grease from make-up and make-up removers is removed and your skin is cooled, toned and feels a little 'tighter'. *Take care not to get the solution in your eyes: if you accidentally splash it in your eyes, rinse out with cold water.*

Soft Skin

Vinegar added to a soaking bath – or even vinegar–soaked 'bandages' wrapped around knees and elbows and left on overnight – are the 'lazy way' to deal with rough or hard skin. In the morning, bathe as usual and gently rub the dry areas with a pumice stone in small circular motions to remove dead skin.

Pleasant Pits

Many commercial antiperspirants contain chemicals and minerals such as zinc to stop you sweating. Many 'natural' deodorants do not stop you sweating but instead mask any body odour with a scent. The antibacterial and deodorizing properties of vinegar can be harnessed by splashing or dabbing a little white vinegar under each arm.

You can even steep a few leaves of herbs – sage is good – in the vinegar if you want a 'scented' lotion (sage is also 'cooling' on the skin). As well as combating odour, the vinegar will not make those white marks on your clothes that many ordinary antiperspirants leave behind. *Do not apply vinegar to broken skin (or after hair removal by shaving) as it will sting!*

Hair

Dandruff

Rinsing your hair with a warm water solution with apple cider vinegar added can help alleviate dandruff. Try a 50:50 solution for an overall 'rinse', or treat a problem area by applying a tablespoon of apple cider vinegar onto the hair and massage gently with your fingertips. Wait a few minutes, then wash as normal and rinse well in warm water. The acetic acid in the vinegar kills the fungus *Malassezia furfur* and restores the pH balance of the scalp.

Remember that too–hot water will make the texture of your hair 'dry' while rubbing your scalp too much will stimulate the sebaceous glands to release their oils, resulting in greasy hair.

Blonde Protection

Blonde hair – whether natural or by design – can need extra protection especially if you swim in chlorinated pools. The chlorine keeps the water safe but it can give blonde hair a greenish tinge so to protect it, rub apple cider vinegar into your hair and let it set for 15 minutes or so before taking the plunge.

Hair Conditioner

Bring the life back into limp or damaged hair with a nourishing hair conditioner. Whip together 1 teaspoon apple cider vinegar

with 2 tablespoons almond
or olive oil and 3 egg whites.

Gently massage the mix into your
hair then cover with a shower cap –
or plastic wrap – for 30 minutes.
Rinse with warm – not hot – water,
unless you want scrambled egg
whites cooked in your hair! Then
shampoo and wash as normal.

Nitty-Gritty

Head lice, known scientifically as
Pediculosis capitis are commonly
associated with school children, but
adults can get them too. Contrary to
popular opinion which implies that
those who get head lice have dirty hair, head lice adore squeaky clean and preferably fine,
straight hair. The lice are keen travellers looking for 'human hotels' and are most often
spread by being transferred between clothing.

While head lice themselves do not transmit disease, unless treated, their itchy infestation
can be embarrassing and make life a misery. The wingless 1-mm lice feed on the scalp and
lay their eggs – the nits – which are each 'glued' to a single hair close to the scalp.

An over the counter preparation will kill the lice, but after shampooing, an extra treatment
rinsing an infected head with white vinegar will dissolve the 'glue' holding the eggs to the
hair which should then be combed out using a very fine-toothed comb. The treatment will
need to be repeated every 4–5 days until the hair is clear of infestation.

Nails

Soften Cuticles

A manicure or pedicure requires attention not only to the nails but to the cuticles as well. Soften cuticles by soaking your fingers and toes in white vinegar for 5 minutes.

Longer Lasting Nail Polish

Nail polish lasts longer if you dampen the nails first with a cotton wool ball soaked in apple cider or white vinegar. Let the nails dry briefly then apply your favourite shade.

Healthy Toenails

While you are pampering your feet, take a moment or two to inspect the condition of your toenails: modern synthetic hosiery, training shoes and wearing closed shoes for days on end where toes are in slightly damp, dark and airless conditions can provide the ideal home for fungal infections which often go unnoticed until they become a real problem.

Give foot fungus the boot with regular footbaths made of 1 part vinegar to 2 parts warm water. Sit back, relax and soak away aching feet safe in the knowledge that they will be deodorized, softened and healthy – perfect for going shoe shopping!

Cookery
& Recipes

The Basics

The wonders of vinegar? Hannibal knew, Hippocrates certainly did and, as we have seen, so did Cleopatra. Records show it was as early as 3000 BC that vinegar was produced commercially and used in every facet of life – as an effective remedy for many ailments, for all kinds of cleaning, for veterinary purposes, as well as being extremely useful both in agriculture and horticulture. But let's not forget its invaluable use in food preparation and flavouring...

Make Vinegar from Scratch

The Mother

First you need the 'vinegar mother': place 2 tablespoons vinegar and half a bottle of wine or cider in a bowl and leave for 2 weeks uncovered in a sunny position. The skin that forms is the 'acetobacter' or 'mother'. This is your starter.

Take Time

Skim off the 'mother' and place it with more of the same wine or cider originally used into a clean bowl, ensuring that the 'mother' remains on top. Cover with muslin, or other porous material that will allow plenty of oxygen through while protecting the liquid from insects. Leave in a warm place for 1 month or longer, until you are happy with the taste.

Strain off the vinegar intro a sterile bottle and cork. Add more alcohol to the 'mother' in order to start again – the 'mother' lasts indefinitely, as long as fresh alcohol is 'fed' to it.

Culinary Tips

Perfect Poached Eggs

Add a few drops of distilled white or white wine vinegar to the water when poaching eggs; this will help to keep the white intact.

No More Cracks

Add 2 teaspoons vinegar to the water when boiling eggs to prevent them from cracking.

Tender Meat

Add 1 tablespoon of a vinegar, such as red wine or cider vinegar, to stews and casseroles to help tenderize the meat. When marinating meat, add 1 tablespoon vinegar to the marinade which again will help to tenderize.

Kill Germs

Lightly wiping raw meat with a little vinegar will help to eradicate bacteria.

Keep Food Longer

Vinegar acts as a preserver – olives when covered in white wine vinegar and kept covered in the refrigerator will keep indefinitely.

Cut Through Grease

When eating fried food, such as chips, sprinkle with a few drops of vinegar to remove the greasy taste and feel to the mouth. Some will argue that it helps your body 'break down the fat' too! (*See* page 104.)

Flavour Enhancer

Add a zing to boring bland dishes by adding 2–3 teaspoons vinegar. Try balsamic and look for the different balsamic flavours.

De-glazing the Pan

Add 1–2 tablespoons vinegar to de-glaze a frying pan or roasting tin. (Adding liquid to the dried and caramelized meat juices in the pan after cooking meat provides a delicious jus or gravy when combined with the meat juices.)

Clean Pudding Pans

When steaming a pudding add a few drops of vinegar to the water in the bottom of the pan. This will keep the pan clean.

Flavoured Vinegars

Recently there has been an explosion of flavoured vinegars available on the market, especially with Balsamic vinegar of which there are now varieties featuring herbs and flowers. Although considered a wine vinegar, it is actually made from grape pressings that have never been permitted to ferment into wine. Its rich, smooth depth of flavour is imparted to the food when used in cooking.

Rosemary Vinegar

Makes 600 ml/1 pint/2½ cups

450 g/1 lb fresh rosemary sprigs, rinsed
600 ml/1 pint/2½ cups white wine or cider vinegar

This recipe can be used with a variety of herbs – try tarragon, thyme, bay and oregano.
The more delicate herbs such as basil, dill, mint and coriander will need their leaves bruising
slightly. Avoid using dried herbs or spices as these could make the vinegar cloudy. For
maximum flavour, if you grow your own rosemary, pick it first thing in the morning after the
dew has dried and before it gets hot. The essential oils are released when it is around 30°C/85°F.

Discard the woody stems from the rosemary and place half in a glass bowl. Pour over the
vinegar, stir, cover lightly and leave in a cool place for 7 days stirring occasionally. Strain,
discarding the rosemary. Repeat with the remaining rosemary and pour the strained vinegar
over. Cover lightly and stir occasionally then leave for a further 7 days. Pour through a fine
sieve into sterilized bottles. Add 2–3 rinsed sprigs of fresh rosemary and screw down tightly.
Store in a dark place.

Rose Vinegar

Makes approx. 600ml/1pint/2½ cups

350 g/12 oz/1½ cups rose petals
approx. 300ml/½ pt/1¼ cups white wine vinegar

This is a delicately flavoured vinegar that is perfect to use as a dressing on salads or vegetables. Make sure that you use rose petals that have a perfume. Petals from other edible flowers can be used in this way too: try chrysanthemums, nasturtiums, marigolds or sweet peas.

Lightly rinse and dry the petals ensuring that there are no insects or bugs. Place in a sterilized 300 ml/½ pint/1¼ cup-glass jar with a screw lid. Do not pack down too firmly. Cover with white wine vinegar, seal and leave in a sunny place for at least 1 month before using.

Spiced Vinegar

Makes 700 ml/1¼ pints/3 cups

6 tsp peppercorns
3 tsp mustard seeds
2 tsp allspice
1 blade mace
1 large cinnamon stick, bruised
4 fresh bay leaves
1 small piece root ginger, chopped
1 tbsp salt
700 ml/1¼ pints/3 cups malt vinegar

This is perfect if wishing to make your own pickles and chutneys. Again you can vary the spices used according to personal preference. White distilled vinegar is often used as it gives a sharper tang, however white wine, red or malt vinegar is fine to use too.

Tie all the spices into a piece of muslin and place in a non-reactive saucepan. Add 230 ml/8 fl oz/1 cup of the vinegar and bring to the boil. Boil for 3 minutes then add the remaining vinegar and boil for a further 3 minutes. Remove from the heat and leave covered for at least 24 hours. Strain into sterilized bottles and screw down.

Dressings & Sauces

Ever had a dish that was boring and uninspiring – yet
looked fabulous? If so here is the answer – simply jazz
it up with a dressing or sauce bursting with flavour.
Dressings and sauces should be quick and easy to
make using the simplest ingredients and yet
give an explosion of taste.

Classic Vinaigrette

Makes 145 ml/5 fl oz/²/₃ cup

4 tbsp olive oil
1½ tbsp white wine vinegar
1–2 tsp sugar, or to taste

freshly ground black pepper to taste
freshly milled rock salt to taste
1 tsp mustard powder
1 tsp caster/superfine gran. sugar, or to taste

This dressing is used universally and can vary immensely according to local tastes and ingredients. Place all the ingredients into a screw top jar and shake until thoroughly blended. Adjust seasoning and sweetness to taste. Use as required. Store in a cool cupboard, not in the refrigerator, as this will make the olive oil go cloudy. If liked, replace the sugar with 1 teaspoon clear honey; replace 1 tablespoon of the vinegar with either balsamic vinegar, red wine vinegar or a herb vinegar; or add 1–2 teaspoons crushed garlic or finely chopped chilli. You can also add 1 tablespoon finely chopped fresh herb.

Hollandaise Sauce

Makes 145 ml/5 fl oz/²/₃ cup

2 tbsp tarragon or white wine vinegar
1 tbsp water
2 fresh medium egg yolks

75–100g/1 stick unsalted butter, cut into
small dice
freshly milled rock salt and freshly ground
black pepper

This is a true classic and is perfect for serving with fish, eggs and vegetables. Boil the vinegar and water together until reduced by about half. Cool, then place the egg yolks in a small bowl and stir in the cooled vinegar solution. Place the bowl over a pan of gently simmering water and heat, whisking until the mixture thickens. Gradually whisk in the butter, whisking well after each addition. Continue until all the butter has been added. Season to taste and if the sauce is too sharp add a little more butter, or if too thick, add a little hot water.

Crème Fraîche Dressing

Makes about 145 ml/5 fl oz/²/₃ cup

85 ml/3 fl oz/¹/₃ cup crème fraîche
2 tsp Dijon mustard or to taste

freshly ground black pepper
4 tbsp extra virgin olive oil
2 tbsp champagne or white wine vinegar

This makes a delicious change from mayonnaise.

Place the crème fraîche, mustard, pepper, olive oil and vinegar in a screw top jar and shake until blended. Use as required. If liked, fromage frais can be used in place of the crème fraîche.

BBQ Sauce

Makes about 145 ml/5 fl oz/²⁄₃ cup

50 g/2 oz/¹⁄₂ stick butter
1 large onion, peeled and finely chopped
1 tsp tomato purée

2 tbsp herb vinegar such as tarragon or rosemary
1–2 tbsp, or to taste, soft brown sugar
2 tsp dry mustard powder
2 tbsp Worcestershire sauce
145 ml/5 fl oz/²⁄₃ cup water

Melt the butter in a saucepan and gently fry the onion for 4 minutes, stirring frequently. Add the tomato purée and continue to fry for 2 minutes. Blend the remaining ingredients together then add to the pan, bring to the boil. Reduce the heat and simmer for 8–10 minutes or until a thick sauce consistency is reached. Use as required.

Mint Sauce

Makes 85 ml/3 fl oz/¹⁄₂ cup

25 g/1 oz/2 tbsp fresh mint sprigs
2 tsp caster/superfine gran. sugar or clear honey

2 tbsp boiling water
2 tbsp white wine vinegar
1 tbsp balsamic vinegar

Ideal to serve with all lamb dishes. Try adding a spoonful or two to a lamb casserole or stew.

Strip off the mint leaves from the stalks and chop finely. Place in a small bowl and add the sugar or honey. Pour over the boiling water, stir well then leave for 5 minutes. Add both vinegars, stir well and pour into a sauce boat. Leave for 1 hour before using.

Preserves & Pickles

Fed up with bland food? Bored with the traditional preserves and chutneys? Feel that your dishes have lost their zing? Well no problem. Using our old friend vinegar, it is really easy to make a delicious, exotic and fantastic chutney to liven up all hot or cold dishes.

Salmon Ceviche

Serves 4

350 g/12 oz fresh salmon fillet, skinned
145 ml/5 fl oz/²/₃ cup lime juice
2 tbsp sherry vinegar
1 tbsp balsamic vinegar
1 bag salad leaves
100 g/4 oz/³/₄ cup cherry tomatoes, halved
small piece cucumber, sliced

Although this is not strictly a preserve in the conventional sense, the vinegar in the recipe preserves the salmon rather than cooking it. Other very fresh fish can be used in this manner – try cod, haddock, monkfish or trout.

1   Lightly rinse the salmon and cut into small cubes; place in a bowl. Blend the lime juice with the vinegars and pour over the salmon. Cover and leave in the refrigerator to marinate for at least 12 hours or overnight if possible. Stir occasionally.
2   When ready to serve, arrange the salad leaves on 4 individual plates and arrange the tomatoes and cucumber on top. Drain the salmon and place on top of the salad and serve.

Mango, Apricot & Cranberry Chutney

Makes about 1.5 kg/3 lb

8 ripe but still firm mangos
450 g/1 lb/c. 5 fresh apricots
225 g/8 oz fresh cranberries
450 g/1 lb/3 cups onions, peeled and chopped
2–4 green chillies, seeded and chopped
3 garlic cloves, peeled and chopped
7.5 cm/3 in-piece root ginger, grated
460 ml/¾ pt/2 cups cider vinegar
550 g/1 lb 4 oz/2½ cups soft light brown sugar
½ tsp salt
juice from 1 large lemon (about 4 tbsp)

You can vary the flavour of this chutney
by using different fruits and vinegar.
Simply use this as your basic recipe.

1   Peel the mangos, discard the stones and roughly chop the flesh. Place in a non–reactive
    preserving or large pan. Stone the apricots, chop roughly and add to the pan together
    with all the remaining ingredients.
2   Place over a gentle heat and heat until the sugar has completely dissolved, stirring
    occasionally.
3   Bring to the boil, reduce the heat to a simmer and cook for 1 hour or until really soft and
    a thick consistency is reached. Taste and adjust sweetness then pot in clean sterilized
    jars. When cold, cover, label and store in a cool dark place for 1 month before using.

Mixed Pickles

Makes 900 g/2 lb/4 cups

900 g/2 lbs/4 cups mixed vegetables such as
cauliflower, broccoli, shallots, cucumber,
French/green beans, courgette/zucchini
and carrots
3 tbsp salt
1 litre/2 pints/4¹/₂ cups spiced vinegar (see page 135)

All manner of vegetables can be used for
this pickle. It is ideal for pickling excess
vegetables when they are in season and
there is a glut.

1   If using cauliflower or broccoli, break into small florets, peel the shallots and cucumber
    and discard the seeds. Trim the beans and wash thoroughly, then chop into small
    pieces. Peel the courgette if using and cut into small chunks. Peel the carrots and dice.
2   Dissolve the salt in 1 litre/2 pints/4¹/₂ cups water. Place all the vegetables in a large bowl
    and pour over the brine. Leave overnight.
3   Next day, rinse thoroughly, rinsing at least 3–4 times to remove any excess salt, then
    drain and dry on clean cloths. Pack into sterilized jars and cover with the vinegar. Cover
    with non reactive lids. label and store in a cool dark place.

Starters, Salads & Side Dishes

If not used carefully, vinegar can swamp the flavour of some foods. This applies particularly with starters and salads which often consist of raw ingredients with a mild delicate flavour that is easily destroyed. One good way to overcome this is to use a vinegar in a dressing or sauce that has been 'aged' and of course to use the correct amount. A mature mellow flavour from an 'aged' vinegar such as balsamic will enhance rather than destroy the dish.

Beetroot & Potato Medley

Serves 4

350 g/12 oz/2 cups raw baby beetroot/beet
$^1/_2$ tsp sunflower oil
5–6 (225 g/8 oz) new potatoes
$^1/_2$ cucumber, peeled
3 tbsp white wine vinegar
150 ml/5 fl oz/$^1/_2$ cup natural yogurt
salt and freshly ground black pepper
fresh salad leaves
1 tbsp freshly snipped chives, to garnish

1   Preheat the oven to 180 C/350 F/Gas Mark 4. Scrub the beetroot thoroughly and place on a baking tray.

2   Brush the beetroot with a little oil and cook for 1$^1/_2$ hours or until a skewer is easily insertable into the beetroot. Allow to cool a little, then remove the skins.

3   Cook the potatoes in boiling water for about 10 minutes. Rinse in cold water and drain. Reserve the potatoes until cool. Dice evenly.

4   Cut the cucumber into cubes and place in a mixing bowl. Chop the beetroot into small cubes and add to the bowl with the reserved potatoes. Gently mix the vegetables together.

5   Mix together the vinegar and yogurt and season to taste with a little salt and pepper. Pour over the vegetables and combine gently.

6   Arrange on a bed of salad leaves, garnish with the snipped chives and serve.

Hot & Spicy Red Cabbage with Apples

Serves 8

900 g/2 lb/9 cups red cabbage, cored and shredded
450 g/1 lb/4 cups onions, peeled and finely sliced
450 g/1 lb/3 cups cooking apples, peeled, cored and
    finely sliced
$^{1}/_{2}$ tsp mixed spice
1 tsp ground cinnamon
2 tbsp light soft brown sugar
salt and freshly ground black pepper
grated rind of 1 large orange
1 tbsp fresh orange juice
50 ml/2 fl oz/$^{1}/_{4}$ cup medium sweet cider
    (or apple juice)
2 tbsp wine or balsamic vinegar

To serve

crème fraîche
freshly ground black pepper

1   Preheat the oven to 150°C/300°F/Gas Mark 2. Put just enough cabbage in a large casserole dish to cover the base evenly.

2   Place a layer of the onions and apples on top of the cabbage.

3   Sprinkle a little of the mixed spice, cinnamon and sugar over the top. Season with salt and pepper.

4   Spoon over a small portion of the orange rind, orange juice and the cider.

5   Continue to layer the casserole dish with the ingredients in the same order until used up.

6   Pour the vinegar as evenly as possible over the top layer of the ingredients.

7   Cover the casserole dish with a close–fitting lid and bake in the preheated oven, stirring occasionally, for 2 hours until the cabbage is moist and tender. Serve immediately with the crème fraîche and black pepper.

French Onion Tart

Serves 4

Quick flaky pastry:
125 g/4 oz/¹/₂ cup butter
175 g/6 oz/1³/₄ cups plain/all-purpose
 flour
pinch of salt

For the filling:
2 tbsp olive oil
4 large onions, peeled and thinly sliced
3 tbsp white wine vinegar
2 tbsp muscovado sugar
a little beaten egg or milk
175 g/6 oz/1¹/₂ cups Cheddar cheese, grated
salt and freshly ground black pepper

1   Preheat the oven to 200 C/400 F/Gas Mark 6. Place the butter in the freezer for 30
    minutes. Sift the flour and salt into a large bowl. Remove the butter from the freezer
    and grate using the coarse side of a grater, dipping the butter in the flour every now
    and again as it makes it easier to grate. Mix the butter into the flour, using a knife,
    making sure all the butter is coated thoroughly with flour.

2   Add 2 tablespoons cold water and continue to mix, bringing the mixture together. Use
    your hands to complete the mixing. Add a little more water if needed to leave a clean
    bowl. Place the pastry in a polythene bag and chill in the refrigerator for 30 minutes.

3   Heat the oil in a large frying pan, then fry the onions for 10 minutes, stirring
    occasionally until softened.

4   Stir in the white wine vinegar and sugar. Increase the heat and stir frequently, for
    another 4–5 minutes until the onions turn a deep caramel colour. Cook for another 5
    minutes, then reserve to cool.

5   On a lightly floured surface, roll out the pastry to a 35.5-cm/14-inch circle. Wrap over a
    rolling pin and move the circle on to a baking sheet.

6   Sprinkle half the cheese over the pastry, leaving a 5-cm/2-inch border around the edge,
    then spoon the caramelized onions over the cheese.

7   Fold the uncovered pastry edges over the edge of the filling to form a rim and brush the
    rim with beaten egg or milk. Season to taste with salt and pepper. Sprinkle over the
    remaining Cheddar and bake for 20–25 minutes. Transfer to a plate and serve immediately.

Panzanella

Serves 4

250 g/9 oz/1 loaf (9 thick slices) day-old
   Italian-style bread
1 tbsp red wine vinegar
4 tbsp olive oil
1 tsp lemon juice
1 small garlic clove, peeled and finely chopped
1 red onion, peeled and finely sliced
1 cucumber, peeled if preferred
2 medium ripe tomatoes, deseeded
150 g/5 oz/$^1/_4$ cup pitted black olives
about 20 basil leaves, coarsely torn or left
   whole if small
sea salt and freshly ground black pepper

1   Cut the bread into thick slices, leaving the crusts on. Add 1 teaspoon red wine vinegar to a jug of iced water, put the slices of bread in a bowl and pour over the water. Make sure the bread is covered completely. Leave to soak for 3–4 minutes until just soft.

2   Remove the soaked bread from the water and squeeze it gently, first with your hands and then in a clean tea towel to remove any excess water. Put the bread on a plate, cover with clingfilm and chill in the refrigerator for about 1 hour.

3   Meanwhile, whisk together the olive oil, the remaining red wine vinegar and lemon juice in a large serving bowl. Add the garlic and onion and stir to coat well.

4   Halve the cucumber and remove the seeds. Chop both the cucumber and tomatoes into 1 cm/$^1/_2$ inch dice. Add to the garlic and onions with the olives. Tear the bread into bite-sized chunks and add to the bowl with the fresh basil leaves. Toss together to mix and serve immediately, with a grinding of sea salt and black pepper.

Chef's Rice Salad

Serves 4

225 g/8 oz/1¼ cups wild rice
½ cucumber
10 cherry tomatoes
6 spring/green onions, trimmed
5 tbsp extra-virgin olive oil
2 tbsp balsamic vinegar
1 tsp Dijon mustard
1 tsp caster sugar
salt and freshly ground black pepper
125 g/4 oz/4 cups rocket/arugula
125 g/4 oz back bacon
125 g/4 oz cooked chicken meat, finely diced
125 g/4 oz Emmenthal/Swiss cheese, grated
125 g/4 oz large cooked prawns/shrimp, peeled
1 avocado, stoned, peeled and sliced, to garnish
warm crusty bread, to serve

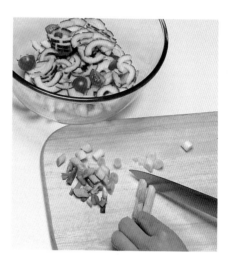

1　Put the rice in a saucepan of water and bring to the boil, stirring once or twice. Reduce the heat, cover and simmer gently for 30–50 minutes, depending on the texture you prefer. Drain well and reserve.

2　Thinly peel the cucumber, cut in half, then using a teaspoon, remove the seeds. Cut the cucumber into thin slices. Cut the tomatoes in quarters. Cut the spring onions into diagonal slices.

3　Whisk the olive oil with the vinegar, then whisk in the mustard and sugar. Season to taste with salt and pepper.

4　In a large bowl, gently toss together the cooled rice with the tomatoes, cucumber, spring onions and the rocket. Pour over the dressing and toss lightly together.

5　Heat a griddle pan and when hot cook the bacon on both sides for 4–6 minutes, or until crisp. Remove and chop. Arrange the prepared rocket salad on a platter, then arrange the bacon, chicken, cheese and prawns on top. Toss, if wished. Garnish with avocado slices and serve with plenty of warm, crusty bread.

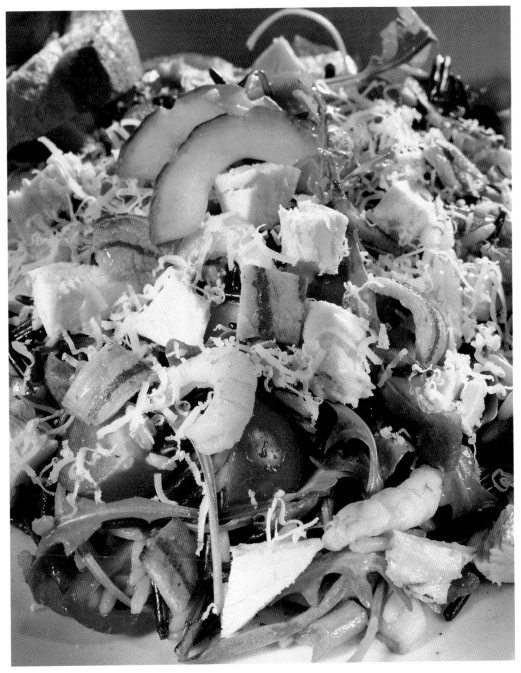

Warm Chicken & Potato Salad with Peas & Mint

Serves 4–6

9–12 (450 g/1 lb) new potatoes, peeled or scrubbed
  and cut into bite-sized pieces
salt and freshly ground black pepper
2 tbsp cider vinegar
175 g/6 oz/1½ cups frozen garden peas, thawed
1 small ripe avocado
4 cooked chicken breasts, about 450 g/1 lb in weight,
  skinned and diced
2 tbsp freshly chopped mint
2 heads small lettuce
fresh mint sprigs, to garnish

For the dressing:

2 tbsp raspberry or sherry vinegar
2 tsp Dijon mustard
1 tsp clear honey
50 ml/2 fl oz/¼ cup sunflower oil
50 ml/2 fl oz/¼ cup extra-virgin olive oil

1 Cook the potatoes in lightly salted boiling water for 15 minutes, or until just tender; do not overcook. Rinse under cold running water to cool slightly, then drain and turn into a large bowl. Sprinkle with the cider vinegar and toss gently.

2 Run the peas under hot water to ensure that they are thawed, pat dry with absorbent kitchen paper and add to the potatoes.

3 Cut the avocado in half lengthways and remove the stone. Peel and cut the avocado into cubes and add to the potatoes and peas. Add the chicken and stir together lightly.

4 To make the dressing, place all the ingredients in a screw-top jar, with a little salt and pepper and shake well to mix; add a little more oil if the flavour is too sharp. Pour over the salad and toss gently to coat. Sprinkle in half the mint and stir lightly.

5 Separate the lettuce leaves and spread onto a large shallow serving plate. Spoon the salad on top and sprinkle with the remaining mint. Garnish with mint sprigs and serve.

Smoked Salmon Sushi

Serves 4

125 g/4 oz/¹⁄₂ cup sushi rice or round
   pudding rice
2 tbsp cider vinegar
1 tbsp caster/superfine gran. sugar
1 tsp salt
2 green leeks, trimmed
225 g/8 oz smoked salmon
1 tsp Japanese soy sauce

To garnish:

few fresh chives
lemon or lime wedges

1   Wash the rice in plenty of cold water, then drain. Put it and 200 ml/7 fl oz cold water in a saucepan and leave to soak for 30 minutes. Place the saucepan over a medium heat and bring to the boil, stirring frequently. Lower the heat, cover and cook for about 15 minutes, or until the grains are tender and the water has been absorbed. Remove from the heat and leave, still covered, for a further 10–15 minutes. Place the vinegar, sugar and salt in a small saucepan. Heat gently, stirring to dissolve the sugar. Turn the rice into a large bowl, sprinkle over the vinegar mixture and mix through the rice.

2   Cut the trimmed leeks in half lengthways, then blanch in boiling water for 3–4 minutes. Drain and place in ice-cold water for 5 minutes, then drain.

3   Separate the leek leaves. Cut both the leek leaves and the salmon slices lengthways into 2.5 x 7.5 cm (1 x 3 inch) strips, reserving 2 wide leek leaves. Place the leek slices neatly on top of the sliced salmon.

4   Spoon the rice onto the salmon and leek slices, then roll into parcels. Using the tip of a sharp knife, slice the reserved leek leaves lengthways into long strips. Tie the strips around the smoked salmon parcels. Sprinkle the parcels with a few drops of the soy sauce, garnish with the chives and lemon wedges and serve.

Seared Scallop Salad

Serves 4

12 king (large) scallops
1 tbsp margarine or butter
2 tbsp orange juice
2 tbsp balsamic vinegar
1 tbsp clear honey
2 ripe pears, washed
125 g/4 oz/4 cups rocket/arugula
125 g/4 oz/4 cups watercress
50 g/2 oz /¹/₂ cup walnuts
freshly ground black pepper

1   Clean the scallops removing the thin black vein from around the white meat and coral. Rinse thoroughly and dry on absorbent kitchen paper.

2   Cut into 2–3 thick slices, depending on the scallop size.

3   Heat a griddle pan or heavy-based frying pan, then when hot, add the margarine or butter and allow to melt.

4   Once melted, sear the scallops for 1 minute on each side or until golden. Remove from the pan and reserve.

5   Briskly whisk together the orange juice, balsamic vinegar and honey to make the dressing and reserve.

6   With a small, sharp knife carefully cut the pears into quarters, core then cut into chunks.

7   Mix the rocket leaves, watercress, pear chunks and walnuts. Pile on to serving plates and top with the scallops.

8   Drizzle over the dressing and grind over plenty of black pepper. Serve immediately.

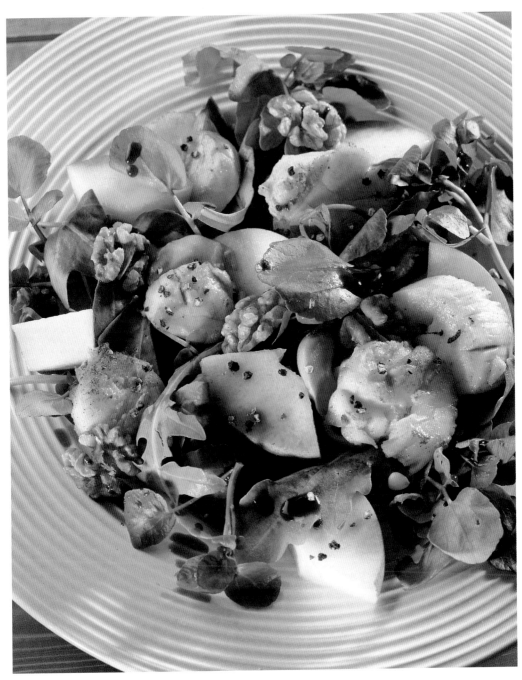

Main Courses

The use of vinegar in main meals goes a step further than in dressings and starters. Here vinegar often plays a dual role, especially in the cooking of meat. To tenderize meat it is marinated in a mixture of vinegar, oil and spices or herbs. Vinegar added during cooking intensifies the depth of flavour. It can also be added at the very end to give a delicious glaze to the finished dish. In the following recipes all manner of vinegars have been used from cider to rice to balsamic.

Bean & Cashew Stir Fry

Serves 4

3 tbsp sunflower oil

1 onion, peeled and finely chopped

1 celery stalk, trimmed and chopped

2.5-cm/1-inch piece fresh root ginger, peeled
and grated

2 garlic cloves, peeled and crushed

1 red chilli, deseeded and finely chopped

175 g/6 oz/1½ cups fine French/green beans,
trimmed and halved

175 g/6 oz/2 cups mangetout/snow peas, sliced
diagonally into 3

75 g/3 oz/½ cup unsalted cashew nuts

1 tsp brown sugar

120 ml/4 fl oz/½ cup vegetable stock

2 tbsp dry sherry

1 tbsp light soy sauce

1 tsp red wine vinegar

salt and freshly ground black pepper

freshly chopped coriander, to garnish

1   Heat a wok or large frying pan, add the oil and when hot, add the onion and celery and
     stir-fry gently for 3–4 minutes or until softened.

2   Add the ginger, garlic and chilli to the wok and stir-fry for 30 seconds. Stir in the French
     beans and mangetout together with the cashew nuts and continue to stir-fry for 1–2
     minutes, or until the nuts are golden brown.

3   Dissolve the sugar in the stock, then blend with the sherry, soy sauce and vinegar. Stir into
     the bean mixture and bring to the boil. Simmer gently, stirring occasionally for 3–4 minutes,
     or until the beans and mangetout are tender but still crisp and the sauce has thickened
     slightly. Season to taste with salt and pepper. Transfer to a warmed serving bowl or spoon
     on to individual plates. Sprinkle with freshly chopped coriander and serve immediately.

Seared Duck with Pickled Plums

Serves 4

4 small skinless, boneless duck breasts
2 garlic cloves, peeled and crushed
1 tsp hot chilli sauce
2 tsp clear honey
2 tsp dark brown sugar
juice of 1 lime
1 tbsp dark soy sauce
6 large plums, halved and stones removed
50 g/2 oz/4 tbsp caster/superfine gran. sugar
50 ml/2 fl oz/¼ cup white wine vinegar
¼ tsp dried chilli flakes
¼ tsp ground cinnamon
1 tbsp sunflower oil
145 ml/5 fl oz/⅔ cup chicken stock
2 tbsp oyster sauce
sprigs of fresh flat leaf parsley, to garnish
freshly cooked noodles, to serve

1 Cut a few deep slashes in each duck breast and place in a shallow dish. Mix together the garlic, chilli sauce, honey, brown sugar, lime juice and soy sauce. Spread over the duck and leave to marinate in the refrigerator for 4 hours or overnight, turning occasionally.

2 Place the plums in a saucepan with the caster sugar, white wine vinegar, chilli flakes and cinnamon and bring to the boil. Simmer gently for 5 minutes, or until the plums have just softened, then leave to cool.

3 Remove the duck from the marinade and pat dry with absorbent kitchen paper. Reserve the marinade. Heat a wok or large frying pan, add the oil and when hot, brown the duck on both sides. Pour in the stock, oyster sauce and reserved marinade and simmer for 5 minutes. Remove the duck and keep warm.

4 Remove the plums from their liquid and reserve. Pour the liquid into the duck sauce, bring to the boil, then simmer, uncovered, for 5 minutes, or until reduced and thickened. Arrange the duck on warmed plates. Divide the plums between the plates and spoon over the sauce. Garnish with parsley and serve immediately with noodles.

Sweet-&-Sour Shredded Beef

Serves 4

350 g/12 oz rump steak
1 tsp sesame oil
2 tbsp Chinese rice wine or sweet sherry
2 tbsp dark soy sauce
1 tsp cornflour
4 tbsp pineapple juice
2 tsp soft light brown sugar
1 tsp sherry vinegar
salt and freshly ground black pepper
2 tbsp groundnut/peanut oil
2 medium carrots, peeled and cut into matchsticks
125 g/4 oz/1½ cups mangetout/snow peas, trimmed
    and cut into matchsticks
1 bunch spring/green onions, trimmed and shredded
2 garlic cloves, peeled and crushed
1 tbsp toasted sesame seeds
freshly cooked Thai fragrant rice, to serve

1   Cut the steak across the grain into thin strips. Put in a bowl with the sesame oil, 1
    tablespoon of the Chinese rice wine or sherry and 1 tablespoon of the soy sauce. Mix
    well, cover and leave to marinate in the refrigerator for 30 minutes.

2   In a small bowl, blend together the cornflour with the remaining Chinese rice wine or
    sherry, then stir in the pineapple juice, remaining soy sauce, sugar and vinegar. Season
    with a little salt and pepper and reserve.

3   Heat a wok until hot, add 1 tablespoon of the oil, then drain the beef, reserving the
    marinade, and stir-fry for 1–2 minutes, or until browned. Remove from the wok and reserve.

4   Add the remaining oil to the wok then add the carrots and stir-fry for 1 minute, then
    add the mangetout peas and spring onions and stir-fry for a further 1 minute.

5   Return the beef to the wok with the sauce, reserved marinade and garlic. Continue
    cooking for 1 minute or until the vegetables are tender and the sauce is bubbling. Turn
    the stir-fry into a warmed serving dish, sprinkle with toasted sesame seeds and serve
    immediately with the Thai fragrant rice.

Creamy Turkey & Tomato Pasta

Serves 4

4 tbsp olive oil
450 g/1 lb turkey breasts, cut into
   bite-sized pieces
550 g/1¼ lb cherry tomatoes, on the vine
2 garlic cloves, peeled and chopped
4 tbsp balsamic vinegar
4 tbsp freshly chopped basil
salt and freshly ground black pepper
200 ml tub (7 fl oz/¾ cup) crème fraîche
350 g/12 oz tagliatelle
shaved Parmesan cheese, to garnish

1   Preheat the oven to 200°C/400°F/Gas Mark 6. Heat 2 tablespoons of the olive oil in a large frying pan. Add the turkey and cook for 5 minutes, or until sealed, turning occasionally. Transfer to a roasting tin and add the remaining olive oil, the vine tomatoes, garlic and balsamic vinegar. Stir well and season to taste with salt and pepper. Cook in the preheated oven for 30 minutes, or until the turkey is tender, turning the tomatoes and turkey once.

2   Meanwhile, bring a large pan of lightly salted water to a rolling boil. Add the pasta and cook according to the packet instructions, or until 'al dente'. Drain, return to the pan and keep warm. Stir the basil and seasoning into the crème fraîche.

3   Remove the roasting tin from the oven and discard the vines. Stir the crème fraîche and basil mix into the turkey and tomato mixture and return to the oven for 1–2 minutes, or until thoroughly heated through.

4   Stir the turkey and tomato mixture into the pasta and toss lightly together. Tip into a warmed serving dish. Garnish with Parmesan cheese shavings and serve immediately.

Spicy Beef Pancakes

Serves 4

50 g/2 oz/¹/₂ cup plain/all-purpose flour
pinch of salt
¹/₂ tsp Chinese five spice powder
1 large egg yolk
145 ml/5 fl oz/²/₃ cup milk
4 tsp sunflower oil
slices of spring/green onion, to garnish

For the spicy beef filling:

1 tbsp sesame oil
4 spring/green onions, sliced
1-cm/¹/₂-inch piece fresh root ginger, peeled and grated
1 garlic clove, peeled and crushed
300 g/11 oz sirloin steak, trimmed and cut into strips
1 red chilli, deseeded and finely chopped
1 tsp sherry vinegar
1 tsp soft dark brown sugar
1 tbsp dark soy sauce

1   Sift the flour, salt and Chinese five spice powder into a bowl and make a well in the centre.
    Add the egg yolk and a little of the milk. Gradually beat in. Whisk in the rest of the milk.

2   Heat 1 teaspoon of the sunflower oil in a small heavy-based frying pan. Pour in just
    enough batter to thinly coat the base of the pan. Cook over a medium heat for 1 minute,
    or until the underside of the pancake is golden brown. Turn or toss the pancake and cook
    for 1 minute, or until the other side of the pancake is golden brown. Make 7 more
    pancakes with the remaining batter. Stack them on a warmed plate, with greaseproof
    paper between each pancake. Cover with tinfoil and keep warm in a low oven.

3   Make the filling. Heat a wok or large frying pan, add the sesame oil and when hot, add
    the spring onions, ginger and garlic and stir-fry for 1 minute. Add the beef strips, stir-fry
    for 3–4 minutes, then stir in the chilli, vinegar, sugar and soy sauce. Cook for 1 minute,
    then remove from the heat. Spoon one-eighth of the filling over one half of each
    pancake. Fold the pancakes in half, then fold in half again. Garnish with a few slices of
    spring onion and serve immediately.

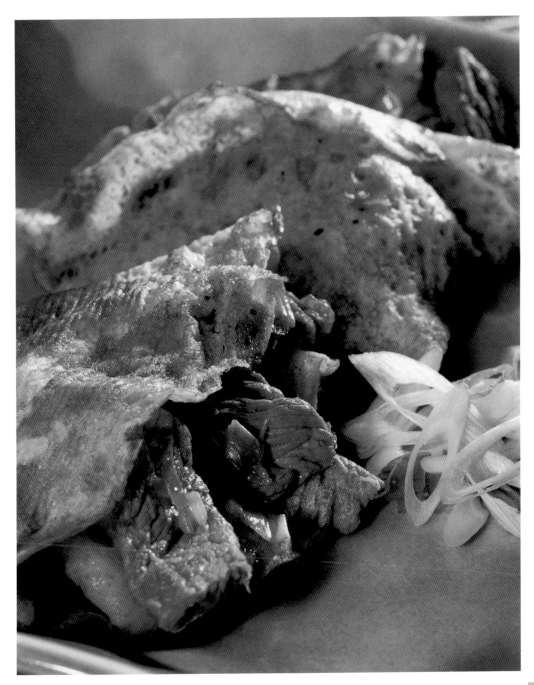

Grilled Steaks with Saffron Potatoes & Roast Tomatoes

Serves 4

13–18 (700 g/1½ lb) new potatoes, halved
few strands of saffron
300 ml/½ pint/1¼ cup vegetable or beef stock
1 small onion, peeled and finely chopped
75 g/3 oz/⅓ cup butter
salt and freshly ground black pepper
2 tsp balsamic vinegar
2 tbsp olive oil
1 tsp caster/superfine gran. sugar
8 plum tomatoes, halved
4 boneless sirloin steaks, each weighing 225 g/8 oz
2 tbsp freshly chopped parsley

1   Cook the potatoes in boiling salted water for 8 minutes and drain well. Return the potatoes to the saucepan along with the saffron, stock, onion and 25 g/1 oz of the butter. Season to taste with salt and pepper and simmer, uncovered for 10 minutes until the potatoes are tender.

2   Meanwhile, preheat the grill to medium. Mix together the vinegar, olive oil, sugar and seasoning. Arrange the tomatoes cut-side up in a foil-lined grill pan and drizzle over the dressing. Grill for 12–15 minutes, basting occasionally, until tender.

3   Melt the remaining butter in a frying pan. Add the steaks and cook for 4–8 minutes to taste and depending on thickness.

4   Arrange the potatoes and tomatoes in the centre of 4 serving plates. Top with the steaks along with any pan juices. Sprinkle over the parsley and serve immediately.

Pan-fried Scallops & Pasta

Serves 4

16 large scallops, shelled
1 tbsp olive oil
1 garlic clove, peeled and crushed
1 tsp freshly chopped thyme
400 g/14 oz/3½ cups penne
4 sun-dried tomatoes in oil, drained and thinly sliced
thyme or oregano sprigs, to garnish

For the tomato dressing:

2 sun-dried tomatoes in oil, drained and chopped
1 tbsp red wine vinegar
2 tsp balsamic vinegar
1 tsp sun-dried tomato paste
1 tsp caster/superfine gran. sugar
salt and freshly ground black pepper
2 tbsp oil from a jar of sun-dried tomatoes
2 tbsp olive oil

1   Rinse the scallops and pat dry on absorbent kitchen paper. Place in a bowl and add the olive oil, crushed garlic and thyme. Cover and chill in the refrigerator until ready to cook.

2   Bring a large pan of lightly salted water to a rolling boil. Add the penne and cook according to the packet instructions, or until 'al dente'.

3   Meanwhile, make the dressing. Place the sun-dried tomatoes into a small bowl or glass jar and add the vinegars, tomato paste, sugar, salt and pepper. Whisk well, then pour into a food processor. With the motor running, pour in the sun-dried tomato oil and olive oil in a steady stream to make a thick, smooth dressing.

4   Preheat a large, dry cast-iron griddle pan over a high heat for about 5 minutes. Lower the heat to medium then add the scallops to the pan. Cook for 1½ minutes on each side. Remove from the pan.

5   Drain the pasta thoroughly and return to the pan. Add the sliced sun-dried tomatoes and dressing and toss. Divide between individual serving plates, top each portion with 4 scallops, garnish with fresh thyme or oregano sprigs and serve immediately.

Roasted Lamb with Rosemary & Garlic

Serves 6

1.6 kg/3½ lb leg of lamb
8 garlic cloves, peeled
few sprigs of fresh rosemary
salt and freshly ground black pepper
4 slices pancetta
4 tbsp olive oil
4 tbsp red wine vinegar
6 medium (900 g/2 lb) potatoes
1 large onion
sprigs of fresh rosemary, to garnish
freshly cooked ratatouille, to serve

1   Preheat oven to 200°C/400°F/Gas Mark 6, 15 minutes before roasting. Wipe the leg of lamb with a clean damp cloth, then place the lamb in a large roasting tin. With a sharp knife, make small, deep incisions into the meat. Cut 2–3 garlic cloves into small slivers, then insert with a few small sprigs of rosemary into the lamb. Season to taste with salt and pepper and cover the lamb with the slices of pancetta.

2   Drizzle over 1 tablespoon of the olive oil and lay a few more rosemary sprigs across the lamb. Roast in the preheated oven for 30 minutes, then pour over the vinegar.

3   Peel the potatoes and cut into large dice. Peel the onion and cut into thick wedges then thickly slice the remaining garlic. Arrange around the lamb. Pour the remaining olive oil over the potatoes, then reduce the oven temperature to 180°C/350°F/Gas Mark 4 and roast for a further 1 hour, or until the lamb is tender. Garnish with fresh sprigs of rosemary and serve immediately with the roast potatoes and ratatouille.

Stir-fried Chicken with Spinach, Tomatoes & Pine Nuts

Serves 4

50 g/2 oz/¹/₂ cup pine nuts
2 tbsp sunflower oil
1 red onion, peeled and finely chopped
450 g/1 lb skinless, boneless chicken
   breast fillets, cut into strips
26 (450 g/1 lb) cherry tomatoes, halved
225 g/8 oz/8 cups baby spinach, washed
salt and freshly ground black pepper
¹/₄ tsp freshly grated nutmeg
2 tbsp balsamic vinegar
50 g/2 oz/¹/₃ cup raisins
freshly cooked ribbon noodles tossed in
   butter, to serve

1   Heat the wok and add the pine nuts. Dry-fry for about 2 minutes, shaking often to ensure that they toast but do not burn. Remove and reserve. Wipe any dust from the wok.

2   Heat the wok again, add the oil and when hot, add the red onion and stir-fry for 2 minutes. Add the chicken and stir-fry for 2–3 minutes, or until golden brown. Reduce the heat, toss in the cherry tomatoes and stir-fry gently until the tomatoes start to disintegrate.

3   Add the baby spinach and stir-fry for 2–3 minutes, or until they start to wilt. Season to taste with salt and pepper, then sprinkle in the grated nutmeg and drizzle in the balsamic vinegar. Finally, stir in the raisins and reserved toasted pine nuts. Serve immediately on a bed of buttered ribbon noodles.

Kung-pao Lamb

Serves 4

450 g/1 lb lamb fillet
2 tbsp soy sauce
2 tbsp Chinese rice wine or dry sherry
2 tbsp sunflower oil
2 tsp sesame oil
50 g/2 oz/¹/₂ cup unsalted peanuts
1 garlic clove, peeled and crushed
2.5 cm/1 inch piece fresh root ginger, finely chopped
1 red chilli, deseeded and finely chopped
1 small green pepper, deseeded and diced
6 spring/green onions, trimmed and diagonally sliced
125 ml/4 fl oz/¹/₂ cup lamb or vegetable stock
1 tsp red wine vinegar
1 tsp soft light brown sugar
2 tsp cornflour
plain boiled or steamed white rice, to serve

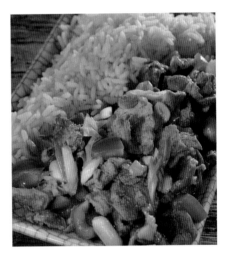

1   Wrap the lamb in baking parchment paper and place in the freezer for about 30 minutes until stiff. Cut the meat across the grain into paper-thin slices. Put in a shallow bowl, add 2 teaspoons of the soy sauce and all the Chinese rice wine or sherry and leave to marinate in the refrigerator for 15 minutes.

2   Heat a wok or frying pan until hot, add the sunflower oil and swirl it around to coat the sides. Add the lamb and stir-fry for about 1 minute until lightly browned. Remove from the wok or pan and reserve, leaving any juices behind.

3   Add the sesame oil to the wok or pan and stir-fry the peanuts, garlic, ginger, chilli, green pepper and spring onions for 1–2 minutes, or until the nuts are golden. Return the lamb with the remaining soy sauce, stock, vinegar and sugar.

4   Blend the cornflour with 1 tablespoon of water. Stir in and cook the mixture for 1–2 minutes, or until the vegetables are tender and the sauce has thickened. Serve immediately with plain boiled or steamed white rice.

Chinese Braised White Chicken with Three Sauces

Serves 4

1.4 kg/3 lb oven-ready chicken
salt
6 spring/green onions, trimmed
5-cm/2-inch piece fresh root ginger, peeled and sliced
2 tsp Szechuan peppercorns, crushed
2¹/₂ tsp sea salt flakes or crushed coarse sea salt
2 tsp freshly grated root ginger
4 tbsp dark soy sauce

4 tbsp sunflower oil
1 tsp caster/superfine gran. sugar
2 garlic cloves, finely chopped
3 tbsp light soy sauce
1 tbsp Chinese rice wine or dry sherry
1 tsp sesame oil
3 tbsp rice vinegar
1 small hot red chilli, deseeded and finely sliced
spring/green onion curls, to garnish
freshly steamed saffron-flavoured rice, to serve

1   Remove any fat from inside the chicken, rub inside and out with ¹/₂ teaspoon salt and leave for 20 minutes. Place 3.4 litres/6 pints water with 2 spring onions and the ginger in a saucepan and bring to the boil. Add the chicken, breast-side down, return to the boil, cover and simmer for 20 minutes. Remove from the heat and leave for 1 hour. Remove the chicken and leave to cool.

2   Dry-fry the Szechuan peppercorns in a non-stick frying pan until they darken slightly and smell aromatic. Crush, mix with the sea salt and reserve.

3   Squeeze the juice from half of the grated ginger, mix with the dark soy sauce, 1 tablespoon of the sunflower oil and half the sugar. Reserve.

4   Finely chop the remaining spring onions and mix with the remaining ginger and garlic in a bowl. Heat the remaining oil to smoking and pour over the onion and ginger. When they stop sizzling, stir in the light soy sauce, Chinese rice wine or sherry and sesame oil. Reserve.

5   Mix together the rice vinegar, remaining sugar and chilli. Stir until the sugar dissolves. Reserve.

6   Remove the skin from the chicken, then remove the legs and cut them in 2 at the joint. Lift the breast meat away from the carcass in 2 pieces and slice thickly crossways. Sprinkle the pepper and salt mixture over the chicken, garnish with spring onion curls and serve with the dipping sauces, spring onion mixture and rice.

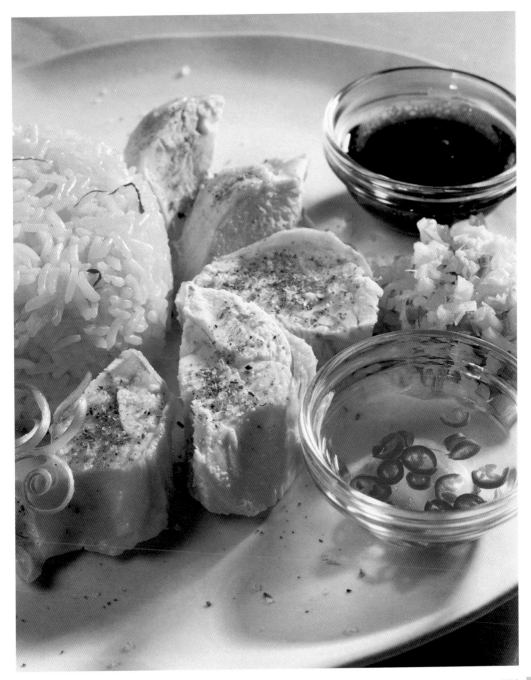

Szechuan Turkey Noodles

Serves 4

1 tbsp tomato paste
2 tsp black bean sauce
2 tsp cider vinegar
salt and freshly ground black pepper
1/2 tsp Szechuan pepper
2 tsp sugar
4 tsp sesame oil
225 g/8 oz dried egg noodles
2 tbsp groundnut/peanut oil
2 tsp freshly grated root ginger
3 garlic cloves, peeled and roughly chopped
2 shallots, peeled and finely chopped
2 courgettes/zucchini, trimmed and cut into
    fine matchsticks
450 g/1 lb turkey breast, skinned and cut into strips
deep-fried onion rings, to garnish

1   Mix together the tomato paste, black bean sauce, cider vinegar, a pinch of salt and
    pepper, the sugar and half the sesame oil. Chill in the refrigerator for 30 minutes.

2   Bring a large saucepan of lightly salted water to the boil and add the noodles. Cook for
    3–5 minutes, drain and plunge immediately into cold water. Toss with the remaining
    sesame oil and reserve.

3   Heat the wok until very hot, then add the oil and when hot, add the ginger, garlic and
    shallots. Stir-fry for 20 seconds, then add the courgettes and turkey strips. Stir-fry for
    3–4 minutes, or until the turkey strips are sealed.

4   Add the prepared chilled black bean sauce and continue to stir-fry for another 4
    minutes over a high heat. Add the drained noodles to the wok and stir until the noodles,
    turkey, vegetables and the sauce are well mixed together. Garnish with the deep-fried
    onion rings and serve immediately.

Pad Thai

Serves 4

225 g/¹/₂ lb flat rice noodles
2 tbsp vegetable oil
225 g/¹/₂ lb boneless chicken breast, skinned, thinly sliced
4 shallots, peeled and thinly sliced
2 garlic cloves, peeled and finely chopped
4 spring/green onions, trimmed, cut into 2-inch pieces
350 g/³/₄ lb fresh white crab meat or tiny prawns/shrimp
75 g/3 oz/1¹/₂ cups fresh bean sprouts, rinsed and drained
2 tbsp preserved or fresh radish, chopped
2–3 tbsp roasted peanuts, chopped (optional)

For the sauce:

3 tbsp Thai fish sauce (nam pla)
2–3 tbsp rice vinegar or cider vinegar
1 tbsp chilli bean or oyster sauce
1 tbsp toasted sesame oil; 1 tbsp light brown sugar
1 red chilli, deseeded and thinly sliced

1   To make the sauce, whisk all the sauce ingredients in a bowl and reserve. Put the rice noodles in a large bowl and pour over enough hot water to cover. Leave to stand for about 15 minutes until softened. Drain and rinse, then drain again.

2   Heat the oil in a wok over a high heat until hot, but not smoking. Add the chicken strips and stir-fry constantly until they begin to colour. Using a slotted spoon, transfer to a plate. Reduce the heat to medium–high.

3   Add the shallots, garlic and spring onions and stir-fry for 1 minute. Stir in the rice noodles, then the reserved sauce; mix well.

4   Add the reserved chicken strips, with the crab meat or prawns, bean sprouts and radish and stir well. Cook for about 5 minutes, stirring frequently, until heated through. If the noodles begin to stick, add a little water.

5   Turn into a large shallow serving dish and sprinkle with the chopped peanuts, if desired. Serve immediately.

Pheasant with Portabella Mushrooms & Red Wine Gravy

Serves 4

25 g/1 oz/1½ tbsp butter
1 tbsp olive oil
2 small pheasants (preferably hens) rinsed, well dried and halved
8 shallots, peeled
300 g/11 oz/3²/₃ cups portabella mushrooms, thickly sliced
2–3 sprigs of fresh thyme or rosemary,

leaves stripped
300 ml/½ pint/1¼ cup Valpolicella or fruity red wine
300 ml/½ pint/1¼ cup hot chicken stock
1 tbsp cornflour
2 tbsp balsamic vinegar
2 tbsp redcurrant jelly, or to taste
2 tbsp freshly chopped flat–leaf parsley
salt and freshly ground black pepper
sprigs of fresh thyme to garnish

1   Preheat the oven to 180°C/350°F/Gas Mark 4. Heat the butter and oil in a large saucepan or frying pan. Add the pheasant halves and shallots, working in batches if necessary, and cook for 10 minutes, or until golden on all sides, shaking the pan to glaze the shallots. Transfer to a casserole dish large enough to hold the pieces in a single layer.

2   Add the mushroom and thyme to the pan and cook for 2–3 minutes, or until beginning to colour. Transfer to the dish with the pheasant halves.

3   Add the wine to the saucepan, it will bubble and steam. Cook, stirring up any browned bits from the pan and allowing to reduce by half. Pour in the stock and bring to the boil, then pour over the pheasant halves. Cover and braise in the preheated oven for 50 minutes, or until tender.

4   Remove the pheasant halves and vegetables to a wide, shallow serving dish and set the casserole over a medium–high heat.

5   Skim off any surface fat and bring to the boil. Blend the cornflour with the vinegar and stir into the sauce with the redcurrant jelly. Boil until the sauce is reduced and thickened slightly. Stir in the parsley and season to taste with salt and pepper. Pour over the pheasant halves, garnish with sprigs of fresh thyme and serve immediately.

Hot Salsa-filled Sole

Serves 4

8 x 175 g/6 oz lemon sole fillets, skinned
145 ml/5 fl oz/²⁄₃ cup orange juice
2 tbsp lemon juice

For the salsa:

1 small mango
8 cherry tomatoes, quartered
1 small red onion, peeled and finely chopped
pinch of sugar
1 red chilli
2 tbsp rice vinegar
zest and juice of 1 lime
1 tbsp olive oil
sea salt and freshly ground black pepper
2 tbsp freshly chopped mint
lime wedges, to garnish
salad leaves, to serve

1   First make the salsa. Peel the mango and cut the flesh away from the stone. Chop finely and place in a small bowl. Add the cherry tomatoes to the mango together with the onion and sugar.

2   Cut the top of the chilli. Slit down the side and discard the seeds and the membrane (the skin to which the seeds are attached). Finely chop the chilli and add to the mango mixture with the vinegar, lime zest, juice and oil. Season to taste with salt and pepper. Mix thoroughly and leave to stand for 30 minutes to allow the flavours to develop.

3   Lay the fish fillets on a board skinned side up and pile the salsa on the tail end of the fillets. Fold the fillets in half, season and place in a large shallow frying pan. Pour over the orange and lemon juice.

4   Bring to a gentle boil, then reduce the heat to a simmer. Cover and cook on a low heat for 7–10 minutes, adding a little water if the liquid is evaporating. Remove the cover, add the mint and cook uncovered for a further 3 minutes. Garnish with lime wedges and serve immediately with the salad.

Sicilian Baked Aubergine

Serves 4

1 large aubergine/eggplant, trimmed
2 celery stalks, trimmed
4 large ripe tomatoes
1 tsp sunflower oil
2 shallots, peeled and finely chopped
1½ tsp tomato purée/paste
25 g/1 oz green pitted olives
25 g/1 oz black pitted olives
salt and freshly ground black pepper
1 tbsp white wine vinegar
2 tsp caster/superfine gran. sugar
1 tbsp freshly chopped basil, to garnish
mixed salad leaves, to serve

1   Preheat the oven to 200°C/400°F/Gas Mark 6. Cut the aubergine into small cubes and place on an oiled baking tray. Cover the tray with tinfoil and bake in the preheated oven for 15–20 minutes until soft. Reserve, to allow the aubergine to cool.

2   Place the celery and tomatoes in a large bowl and cover with boiling water. Remove the tomatoes from the bowl when their skins begin to peel away. Remove the skins then, deseed and chop the flesh into small pieces.

3   Remove the celery from the bowl of water, finely chop and reserve.

4   Pour the vegetable oil into a non–stick saucepan, add the chopped shallots and fry gently for 2–3 minutes until soft. Add the celery, tomatoes, tomato purée and olives. Season to taste with salt and pepper.

5   Simmer gently for 3–4 minutes. Add the vinegar, sugar and cooled aubergine to the pan and heat gently for 2–3 minutes until all the ingredients are well blended. Reserve to allow the aubergine mixture to cool. When cool, garnish with the chopped basil and serve cold with salad leaves.

Seared Tuna with Italian Salsa

Serves 4

4 x 175 g/6 oz tuna or swordfish steaks
salt and freshly ground black pepper
3 tbsp Pernod; 2 tbsp olive oil
zest and juice of 1 lemon
2 tsp fresh thyme leaves
2 tsp fennel seeds, lightly roasted
4 sun-dried tomatoes, chopped
1 tsp dried chilli flakes
assorted salad leaves, to serve

For the salsa:

1 white onion, peeled and finely chopped
2 tomatoes, deseeded and sliced
2 tbsp freshly shredded basil leaves
1 red chilli, deseeded and finely sliced
3 tbsp extra-virgin olive oil
2 tsp balsamic vinegar; 1 tsp caster/superfine gran. sugar

1   Wipe the fish and season lightly with salt and pepper, then place in a shallow dish. Mix together the Pernod, olive oil, lemon zest and juice, thyme, fennel seeds, sun-dried tomatoes and chilli flakes and pour over the fish. Cover lightly and leave to marinate in a cool place for 1–2 hours, occasionally spooning the marinade over the fish.

2   Meanwhile, mix all the ingredients for the salsa together in a small bowl. Season to taste with salt and pepper, then cover and leave for about 30 minutes to allow all the flavours to develop.

3   Lightly oil a griddle pan and heat until hot. When the pan is very hot, drain the fish, reserving the marinade. Cook the fish for 3–4 minutes on each side, taking care not to overcook them – the tuna steaks should be a little pink inside. Pour any remaining marinade into a small saucepan, bring to the boil and boil for 1 minute. Serve the steaks hot with the marinade, chilled salsa and a few assorted salad leaves.

Desserts

It may seem a little strange to have a dessert chapter in a vinegar book. However, there are a few recipes where the addition of vinegar plays an important role. Perhaps the most notable is the Fluffy Meringue, where it has been used to ensure that the meringue has just the correct amount of soft fluffy, marshmallow texture that is required. Vinegar also works wonders for other desserts helping to intensify the flavours of both raw and cooked fruits.

Fluffy Meringue

Makes one 18-cm/
7-inch case

2 medium egg whites
100 g/4 oz/¹/₂ cup caster/superfine gran. sugar
1 tsp raspberry vinegar
1 tsp vanilla extract

Although only a little vinegar is used here, it is surprising what a difference it makes.

Preheat the oven to 150°C/fan oven 130°C/300°F/Gas Mark 2 and line a baking sheet with non-stick baking paper. Mark an 18-cm/7-inch circle on the paper. Whisk the egg whites until stiff then gradually whisk in the sugar a spoonful at a time. When all the sugar has been added stir in the vinegar with the vanilla extract. Place in the centre of the drawn circle and shape into a large case. Bake in the preheated oven for 1¹/₂ hours or until set and firm to the touch. Remove from the oven, leave until cold before using or storing in an airtight tin.

Mango Sorbet

Serves 6

2 large ripe mangos
2 tbsp white wine vinegar
4–5 tbsp. or to taste.
   icing/confectioner's sugar
1 medium egg white

Other fruits can be used for this recipe if liked – try ripe papaya or one of the many varieties of melon. Which ever you use do ensure that the fruits are ripe to get the maximum flavour.

Turn the freezer to rapid freeze. Peel, stone and then roughly chop the mango flesh. Place in a food processor with the vinegar and sugar then blend to a purée. Scrape into a container and freeze for 4 hours or until semi frozen. Whisk the egg white until stiff then stir into the sorbet. Return to the freezer and continue to freeze for 1–2 hours. Allow to soften for 15–30 minutes before serving in scoops.

Balsamic Flavoured Strawberries

Give your guests a surprise by not telling them what you have sprinkled over the fruit and see how many guess.

Hull and lightly rinse some large strawberries and cut in half or quarters. Place in a glass bowl. Pour over 2–3 tablespoons balsamic vinegar. Allow to stand for 1–5 minutes. Sprinkle with 1–2 tablespoons caster/superfine granulated sugar. Stir and serve with ice cream

More Dessert Tips

- Try adding a teaspoon to jelly to give a firmer set.

- Paint a little over a pie crust for extra shine.

- Give extra tang to a lemon tart with a few drops of vinegar.

Vinegar Tips
for Kids

Fun Science for Kids

On a rainy day when children cannot play in the garden or go to the park, amaze and amuse them with some fun science and activities. All of the experiments here are safe and use household items that are probably already in your kitchen cupboards. They are a great way to learn about chemistry, physics and even about the environment.

Coloured Easter Eggs

This is great for kids of all ages. You can either hard or soft boil the eggs for a fun breakfast or snack, or use 'blown' eggshells made as follows: take a medium size egg and gently pierce a hole in each end of the egg with a safety pin; blow hard through one hole so the egg comes out of the other.

To make the paint, mix 1 teaspoon vinegar with each $\frac{1}{2}$ cup of hot water, then add a few drops of food colouring. (Check the food dye bottles for specific amounts.) Vinegar keeps the food dyes bright and prevents streaky, uneven colours.

Berry Ink

Learn how artists in the Middle Ages made inks for manuscripts. All you need is a handful of ripe (or over-ripe) berries (blueberries, cherries, blackberries, strawberries, elderberries, raspberries etc.), $\frac{1}{2}$ teaspoon vinegar and $\frac{1}{2}$ teaspoon salt. Fill a strainer with the berries and hold it over a bowl. Using the rounded back of a wooden spoon, crush the berries against the strainer so that the berry juice strains into the bowl.

Keep adding berries until most of their juice has been strained out and only pulp remains. Add the salt and vinegar to the berry juice. The vinegar helps the ink retain its colour and the salt keeps it from getting too mouldy. If the berry ink is too thick, add a tablespoon of water. Store in a jar with a screw top lid. Only make a small amount of berry ink at a time and, when not in use, keep it tightly covered.

Inflate a balloon

Using a funnel, add 3 teaspoons bicarbonate of soda to a balloon. Fill a small clean bottle ⅓ full with vinegar. Carefully holding the neck of the balloon – and without letting any of the bicarbonate of soda fall into the bottle, fit the balloon over the neck of the bottle. Now hold up the balloon so the bicarbonate of soda falls into the vinegar. Watch as the two mix in the bottle to make carbon dioxide to inflate the balloon.

Volcanic Eruption

This is another fun way to see the chemical reaction of vinegar and bicarbonate of soda. First, make the 'cone' of the volcano. Mix 720 g/1½ lb/6 cups flour, 600 g/1⅓ lb/2 cups salt, 4 tablespoons cooking oil and 460 ml/¾ pt/2 cups water. The resulting mixture should be a smooth, firm dough (add more water if needed). Stand a pop bottle in a baking tray and mould the dough around it into a volcano shape. Fill up the bottle most of the way with warm water (a drop or two of red food colouring added will make a great 'lava' effect!). Add 6 drops of washing-up liquid to the bottle contents. Add 2 tablespoons of bicarbonate of soda to the liquid. Slowly pour in some vinegar (do not waste expensive balsamic vinegar though!) into the bottle and watch the volcano erupt!

Mini Rocket

This is a fun experiment to try for 5 November. Find an old cork – you will need one that fits snugly into your bottle – and glue some streamers on to one end. (Try cutting a few thin 'shreds' from a plastic shopping bag.) Take a small, clean pop or water bottle and pour in 120 ml/4 fl oz/¹/₂ cup each of water and vinegar. Next take a paper towel and put 1 teaspoon of bicarbonate of soda in the centre and twist the ends to stop the 'bicarb' from falling out. Take the bottle outside, and drop in the paper towel with the bicarb in it and put the cork on tight. Stand back and watch the carbon dioxide gas force the cork (with its streamers) out of the bottle.

Bendy Bones

This is a great way to show kids the importance of calcium in their diet to build healthy bones and teeth. Take a chicken bone and place it in a screw top jar of vinegar tightly sealed for a day or so – get your kids to handle the bone before the experiment so they can feel the hardness. When you take the bone out of the vinegar, it will be bendy and rubbery. Why? The vinegar has dissolved the calcium in the bone, making it weak and bendy.

Why We Need to Brush our Teeth

This experiment takes a couple of days, but is a great way to show kids the importance of teeth brushing: eggshells and teeth can both be weakened by acids but protection can be given by fluoride toothpaste. Here's how to do it: take 2 fresh eggs with no cracks in the shells and place one in a jar full of vinegar (a weak acid similar to that which causes tooth cavities) and put the lid on. You will soon start to see bubbles form on the eggshell as the acid starts to work dissolving the calcium.

Take the other egg and carefully smear a good layer of fluoride toothpaste all over the shell, making sure there are no gaps or air bubbles in the toothpaste. Put this egg into a jar filled with vinegar and put the lid on. Let both eggs sit for about 4 days, and then gently lift the eggs out of the jars. The 'unprotected egg' will be very fragile because the acid has eaten into the calcium in the eggshell. Gently rinse off the toothpaste from the 'protected egg' and see how the shell has remained hard thanks to the protective layer of fluoride toothpaste.

Index